AF294330

KNOWLEDGE-BASED SOFTWARE ENGINEERING

edited by

Dorothy Setliff
University of Pittsburgh

Howard Reubenstein
Concept Five Technologies

A Special Issue of
AUTOMATED SOFTWARE ENGINEERING
An International Journal
Volume 4, No. 1 (1997)

SPRINGER SCIENCE+BUSINESS MEDIA, LLC

AUTOMATED
SOFTWARE
ENGINEERING

An International Journal

Volume 4, No. 1, January 1997

Special Issue: Knowledge-Based Software Engineering
Guest Editors: Dorothy Setliff and Howard Reubenstein

Library of Congress Cataloging-in-Publication Data

A C.I.P. Catalogue record for this book is available
from the Library of Congress.

ISBN 978-1-4757-8306-3   ISBN 978-0-585-34714-1 (eBook)
DOI 10.1007/978-0-585-34714-1

Printed on acid-free paper.

Automated Software Engineering, 4, 5 (1997)

Introduction

This special issue of the Journal of Automated Software Engineering contains four extended papers from the 10th Knowledge-Based Software Engineering Conference. The Knowledge-Based Software Engineering Conference provides a forum for researchers and practitioners to discuss applications of automated reasoning, knowledge representation and artificial intelligence techniques to software engineering problems. This conference focuses on specific knowledge-based techniques for constructing, representing, reasoning with, and understanding software artifacts and processes. These techniques may be fully automatic, may support, or cooperate with humans.

Paper session topics include Synthesis, Formal Methods, Knowledge-Based Environments, Process, Reuse/Reengineering, and Program Understanding. The conference was held in November 1995 at the Boston Back Bay Hilton. Despite the U.S. Government shutdown on the last day of the conference (necessitating the departure of some attendees), the conference provided an excellent snapshot of the KBSE field.

The papers in this issue represent the best paper award winners and those identified as strong candidates for best paper. The papers by Dick and Santen and by Ledru report on the application of the Kestrel Institute's KIDS system and software synthesis approach by independent research groups. The application and transfer of the powerful KIDS technology bodes well for the ultimate transfer of KBSE technology into more active use. The paper by Johnson and Erdem also reports on an integration and transfer of technology this time in the form of a software understanding system based on Reasoning Systems' Refinery^{TM} tools with presentation delivered over the World Wide Web. The paper by Howe, Mayrhauser, and Mraz reports on the application of the University of Washington UCPOP planner to generating software test cases using a robot tape library controller as an example problem domain. A final paper, titled "META-AMPHION: Synthesis of Efficient Domain-Specific Program Synthesis Systems" by Michael Lowry and Jeffrey van Baalen describes improvements on the Amphion composition system. This paper was originally submitted and accepted for publication in this special issue, but due to time constraints and page budgets, it will appear in the next issue.

We would like to take this final opportunity to thank everyone who helped make KBSE-10 a success. We hope you enjoy this opportunity to revisit these popular topics in more detail. Information on the Knowledge-Based Software Engineering conferences (either past, present, or future) can be found on the World Wide Web at http://sigart.acm.org/Conferences/kbse.

Howard Reubenstein, hbr@concept5.com
General Chair, Concept Five Technologies

Dorothy Setliff, setliff@ee.pitt.edu
Program Chair, University of Pittsburgh

Automated Software Engineering 4, 7–31 (1997)

Searching for a Global Search Algorithm

SABINE DICK   sab@informatik.uni-bremen.de
Universität Bremen, FB3, Informatik, Bibliothekstraßet, D-28359 Bremen, Germany

THOMAS SANTEN   santen@first.gmd.de
German National Research Center for Information Technology (GMD FIRST), Rudower Chaussee 5, D-12489 Berlin, Germany

Abstract.   We report on a case study to assess the use of an advanced knowledge-based software design technique with programmers who have not participated in the technique's development. We use the KIDS approach to algorithm design to construct two global search algorithms that route baggage through a transportation net. Construction of the second algorithm involves extending the KIDS knowledge base. Experience with the case study leads us to integrate the approach with the spiral and prototyping models of software engineering, and to discuss ways to deal with incomplete design knowledge.

Keywords: formal methods, KIDS, program synthesis, scheduling

1.   Introduction

Advanced techniques to support software construction will only be widely accepted by practitioners if they can be successfully used by software engineers who were not involved in their development and did not receive on-site training by their inventors. Experience has to be gained how knowledge-based methods can be integrated into the practical software engineering process.

We report on experience with the application of the approach to algorithm design underlying the *Kestrel Interactive Development System* (KIDS) (Smith, 1990) to the construction of control software for a simplified baggage transportation system at an airport. In this paper, we use the term *KIDS approach* to denote the concepts that have been implemented in the system KIDS. We did not use the implemented system KIDS in the case study, because we wanted to assess the approach rather than the system. In this way, we could exactly observe how concepts of the approach were used in the case study, and could modify the approach where necessary.

The KIDS system has been applied to a number of case studies at Kestrel Institute. In particular, it has been used in the design of a transportation scheduling algorithm with impressive performance (Smith and Parra, 1993; Smith et al., 1995). We wished to find out if we were able to use this method based on the available publications and produce satisfactory results with reasonable effort. A second goal of this work has been to study how a knowledge-based approach can be integrated into the overall software engineering process. As a case study we chose a non-trivial abstraction of a practically relevant problem to make our experience transferable to realistic applications.

In the following, we elaborate on two issues: a process model we found useful to support application of the KIDS approach, and the merits and shortcomings of the approach we encountered when we explored alternative solutions to the transportation scheduling problem.

We have integrated the spiral and prototyping models of software engineering (Boehm, 1988) with the KIDS approach. We developed the first formal specification and a prototype implementation in parallel. The prototype served to validate the specification and to improve understanding of the problem domain.

In the KIDS approach, global search algorithms are constructed by specializing global search theories that abstractly describe the shape of the search tree set up by the algorithm. For the case study, we wished to explore two alternative search ideas. While we found a theory suitable for the first one in the literature; the second one could not be realized with the documented design knowledge. This led us to develop a new global search theory that needs a slightly modified specialization procedure.

In Section 2, we introduce the baggage transportation problem. Section 3 provides a brief review of the global search theory and the KIDS approach. We present its integration into a process model in Section 4. The design of two transportation schedulers is described in Section 5. Optimizations are sketched in Section 6, where we also discuss the resulting algorithms. Related work is described in Section 7, and we summarize our experience with the approach in Section 8.

2. Baggage transportation scheduling

We wish to develop a controller for the baggage transportation system at an airport. Baggage is transported from check-in counters to gates, from gates to other gates, or from gates to baggage delivery points. Each bag should arrive at its destination in due time.

To simplify the problem, we do not consider on-line scheduling of a continuous flow of baggage fed into the system at the check-in counters, but schedule all baggage checked-in at a particular point in time.

2.1. *Domain model*

We model the transportation net as a directed graph as shown in figure 1. Check-in counters and baggage delivery counters, gates and switches are represented by nodes. We classify these in three kinds: *input nodes*, *transportation nodes* and *output nodes*. Check-in counters correspond to input nodes, switches to transportation nodes and baggage delivery counters to output nodes. Since gates serve to load and unload airplanes, we represent them by an input and an output node.

The edges of the graph model conveyor belts. The *capacity* of a belt is the maximum amount of baggage, the "total weight", that it can carry at a time. Its *duration* is the time it takes to carry baggage from the start to the end node.

Bags are described by their *weight*, *source* and *destination* nodes, and their *due time*. Source and destination are input and output nodes, respectively. Weight and due time are

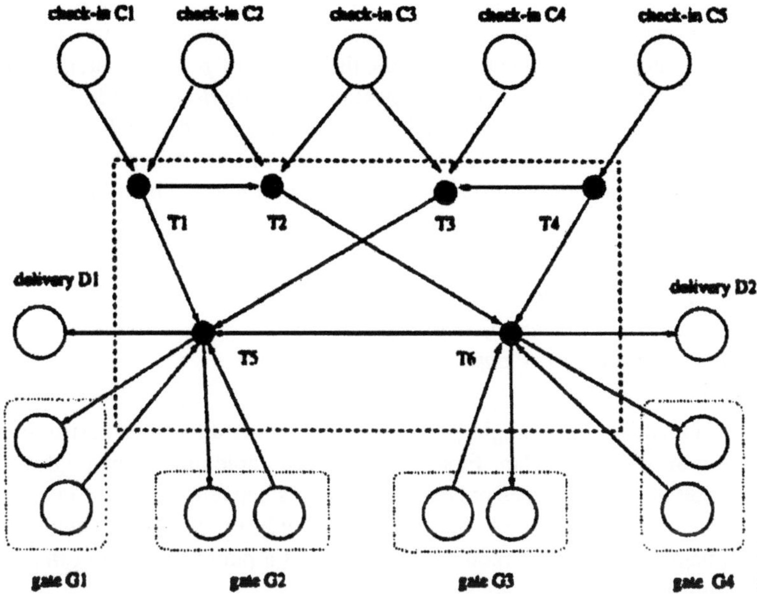

Figure 1.   Transportation network.

positive natural numbers. Due times are specified relative to the beginning of the transportation process.

2.2.   *Problem specification*

We basically use the specification language of (Smith, 1990) which is sorted first order predicate logic. For notational convenience, we use simple polymorphism and higher-order functions in some places, and we also assume predefined sorts for standard data types such as the natural numbers, sets, and lists. Free variables in formulas are implicitly universally quantified and we leave out type information if it is clear from the context.

Our task is to assign, to each bag, a route through the network leading from its source to its destination node in due time. To keep things simple, we require an *acyclic* network without depots at the transportation nodes. Thus, the only way to resolve scheduling conflicts that arise if capacities of conveyor belts are exceeded is to delay baggage at source nodes. A *route* therefore is a pair of a delay and a *path* through the network. We model paths by sequences of vertices. A *plan* maps baggage to routes. We introduce abbreviations for these sorts, where $map(A, B)$ is the sort of all finite mappings from A to B.

$$
\begin{aligned}
path &= seq(vertex) \\
route &= nat \times path \\
plan &= map(baggage, route)
\end{aligned}
$$

Attempting to find a plan for a particular set of bags makes sense only if there exists a *feasible path* for each bag. This is a path p through the network g leading from the source node to the destination node of a bag b, i.e. the first vertex of p is the source node $source(b)$ of b and the last vertex of p is equal to the destination node $dest(b)$ of b. Furthermore, the capacities of all conveyor belts on the path must be at least as big as the weight of the bag b. This is expressed by the predicate $path\_can\_carry(g, p, b)$. A bag for which no feasible path exists cannot be scheduled through the transportation net. The notion of feasibility is formalized by the following equivalence.

$$
\begin{aligned}
feasible\_path(g, b, p) \Longleftrightarrow{}& \\
is\_path(g, p) \wedge{}& source(b) = first(p) \\
\wedge\, dest(b) ={}& last(p) \wedge path\_can\_carry(g, p, b)
\end{aligned}
\tag{1}
$$

Feasibility considers only single paths of a plan. Two additional restrictions refer to the interaction of routes in a plan. First, a plan is acceptable only if the total weight of the bags on any belt at any time does not exceed the belt's capacity, which is expressed by the predicate $capacity\_bounded(g, p)$. Second, we are only interested in complete plans that schedule all baggage. Thus we require the domain of a plan to consist of the entire set of bags bs that must be scheduled, $bs = dom(p)$.

An ideal solution is a plan with feasible paths where all bags arrive at their destination nodes in time and it is not necessary to delay any bags at their source nodes. Although an ideal plan does not exist in general, we must find some plan as long as feasible paths exist for all bags to schedule. Thus, we have to find an optimality criterion to select a most appropriate plan with feasible paths.

For our problem, punctuality is most important, while it is desirable to minimize delays of bags at source nodes and thereby reduce storage space needed at the input counters. We consider punctuality and delays only in a qualitative way, and define a *cost* function based on the criteria if all bags are delivered in time and if baggage is delayed at input nodes.

cost	all bags in time	no delays
0	yes	yes
1	yes	no
2	no	yes
3	no	no

Imagine we have a suitcase b_1 at check-in counter C_1 and another one b_2 at gate G_4 in figure 1. Both have weight 1. They are checked in for the same flight, leaving from gate G_2. Let the transportation time of each belt be one time unit and its capacity also be one unit. A valid transportation plan maps b_1 and b_2 to undelayed routes, where the paths through the net are described by sequences of nodes.

$$
p = \begin{pmatrix} b_1 \mapsto (0, \langle C_1, T_1, T_2, T_6, T_5, G_2 \rangle) \\ b_2 \mapsto (0, \langle G_4, T_6, T_5, G_2 \rangle) \end{pmatrix}
$$

Function *transport_plan(bs : set(baggage), g : graph)*
 where *acyclic(g)* $\land$ $\forall b \in bs.$ $\exists p.$ *feasible_path(g, b, p)*
 returns $(p : plan \mid min(cost, p, \{q \mid bs = dom(q) \land capacity\_bounded(g, q)$
$\land \forall b \in dom(q). feasible\_path(g, b, snd(q(b)))\}))$

Figure 2.   Problem specification.

Now suppose suitcase b_1 shall be transported from C_4 to G_2. As we have to avoid exceeding the capacity of the belt leading to G_2, one possible solution is to delay b_1 by one time unit. This gives us the transportation plan:

$$p = \begin{pmatrix} b_1 \mapsto (1, \langle C_4, T_3, T_5, G_2 \rangle) \\ b_2 \mapsto (0, \langle G_4, T_6, T_5, G_2 \rangle) \end{pmatrix}$$

With the predicates defined so far, we can set up the problem specification as shown in figure 2. We wish to synthesize a function called *transport-plan* with two input parameters, a set of baggage *bs* and a graph *g*. The **where**-clause describes the precondition of the function: we may assume that *g* is acyclic and that there is a feasible path in *g* for all bags in *bs*. The **returns**-clause describes the postcondition for the result of *transport-plan*. The predicate $min(f, x, s)$ is true if x is a member of the set s such that $f(x)$ is a minimum of the image of s under f. Thus, *transport-plan* has to select a plan p with minimal *cost* from the set of all plans q that are complete, do not put more load on belts than allowed, and where the path assigned to each bag b is feasible. This path is the second component $snd(q(b))$ of the route assigned to b under plan q.

3.   Design of global search algorithms

The basic idea of algorithm design in the KIDS approach is to represent design knowledge in design theories. Such a theory is a logical characterization of problems that can be solved by an algorithmic paradigm like "divide and conquer" or "global search". Algorithm design consists of showing that a given problem is an instance of a design theory. In the following, we summarize how global search algorithms are developed in the KIDS approach. For a full account, we refer the reader to (Smith and Lowry 1989; Smith, 1987; Smith, 1990).

Note that the theory of global search algorithms has been developed at Kestrel for nearly a decade. Our work is based on information drawn from several publications which reflect different stages of the theory's development. The account of global search presented in this paper therefore is not a verbatim citation but we have made several minor changes.

3.1.   Design theory

The logical frameworks used in the KIDS approach are algebraic specifications or *theories*, and mappings between them. Theories consist of a *signature* and a list of *axioms* over the signature. The signature declares sorts and functions with their sorts. The axioms describe properties of the functions introduced in the signature. A *signature morphism* maps the sort and function symbols of one specification to expressions over the sorts and functions of another specification such that the sorts of the target expressions are consistent with the sorts of the source symbols. A signature morphism is called a *theory morphism* if the images of the axioms of the source theory are theorems in the target theory, i.e. they are logically entailed by the axioms of the target theory.

The class of problems we deal with is to synthesize a function that is correct with respect to a specification of its input/output behavior. A quadruple $\mathcal{P} = \langle D, R, I, O \rangle$ is called a *problem specification* if the following conditions hold. The sorts D and R describe the input domain and the output range of the function. The predicate $I : D \rightarrow Bool$ describes the admissible inputs and $O : D \times R \rightarrow Bool$ describes the input/output behavior. A function $f : D \rightarrow R$ is a solution to a problem $\mathcal{P}$ if

$$\forall x : D.I(x) \Longrightarrow O(x, f(x)) \tag{2}$$

The problem specification of the transportation problem is described by the following signature morphism:

$$
\begin{aligned}
&f \mapsto transport\_plan \\
&D \mapsto set(baggage) \times graph \\
&R \mapsto plan \\
&I \mapsto \lambda\langle bs, g\rangle. \, acyclic(g) \wedge \forall b \in bs. \, \exists p. \, feasible\_path(g, b, p) \\
&O \mapsto \lambda\langle bs, g\rangle, p. \, min(cost, p, \\
&\qquad\qquad\quad \{q \mid bs = dom(q) \wedge capacity\_bounded(g, q) \\
&\qquad\qquad\quad \wedge \forall b \in dom(q). \, feasible\_path(g, b, snd(q(b)))\})
\end{aligned}
\tag{3}
$$

There is an obvious translation from figure 2 to this morphism. The cartesian product of the input parameters' sorts becomes the input domain D while R becomes the sort of the result in the **returns**-clause. The predicate of this clause is transformed into a function from $D \times R$ to $Bool$ by λ-abstraction over the pair of input parameters and the result.

The synthesis problem is solved if we find an expression for *transport_plan* such that the translation of formula (2) is a theorem under the theory of baggage and graphs.

A *design theory* extends a problem specification by additional functions. It states properties of these functions sufficient to provide a schematic algorithm that correctly solves the problem.

The basic idea of "global search" is to split *search spaces* containing candidate solutions into "smaller" ones until solutions are directly extractable. In this way, a global search algorithm constructs a search tree in which nodes represent search spaces and the children of a node are representations of its subspaces. Solutions may be extractable from each node of the tree, and the set of all solutions extractable from nodes of the tree is the set of all solutions to the search problem.

Let us consider an example. We wish to find a total mapping from the set $U = \{a, b\}$ to the set $V = \{c, d\}$ that fulfills some predicate O and is optimal with respect to some cost function c. Global search can be used to solve this problem as is illustrated in figure 3. The idea is to generate *all* total mappings from U to V, collect the ones that fulfill O and find one of these that has minimal cost.

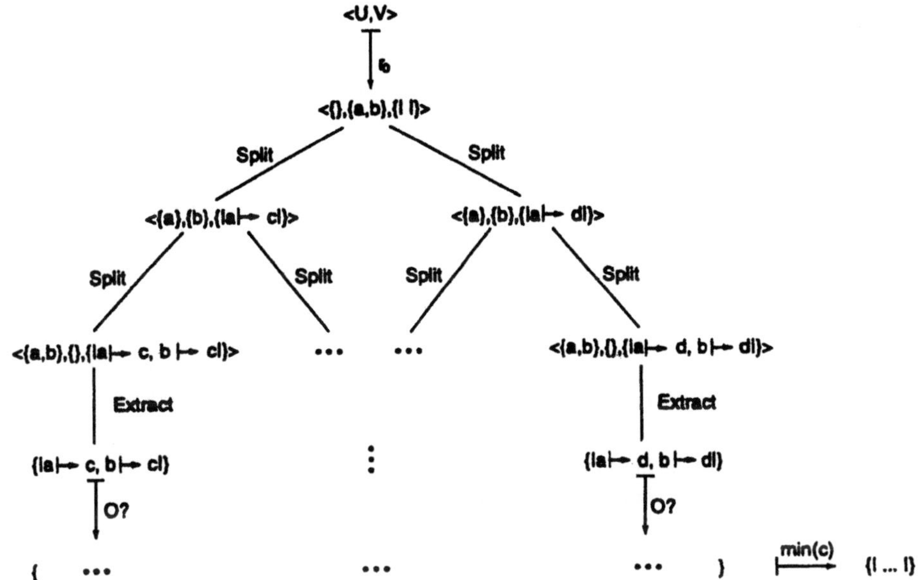

Figure 3. Global search for finite mappings.

Search spaces can be described by triples $\langle S, T, M \rangle$ where S and T partition U and M is a mapping from S to V. The set T contains the elements of U to which nothing has yet been assigned. In order to find all mappings from U to V, the initial search space which becomes the root of the search tree must be $\langle \{\}, U, \{| |\} \rangle$, where $\{| |\}$ is the empty mapping. The initial search space is constructed from the input by the function $\hat{r}_0$. Search is performed by splitting search spaces as long as T is not empty. The predicate *Split* relates a search space to its direct subspaces. They are obtained by picking arbitrary elements of T and V, and extending M by the corresponding maplet. The predicate *Extract* relates a search space descriptor to all solutions that are directly extractable from it. In our example, only the leaves of the search tree contain directly extractable solutions, namely the total mappings M. So far, we have only generated all mappings from U to V but not checked if they fulfill O. This is done after extracting solutions, and finally we pick one of these that is minimal with respect to the cost function c. The search tree of figure 3 shows the search idea for our example, and a global search theory for finite mappings which we present in Section 5.1 formalizes this idea.

For a concrete problem where O and c are known, there are many possibilities for optimization. It may be possible to prune branches of the search tree if they cannot contain feasible solutions, and the search can be terminated if we can decide on the optimality of a solution without inspecting all of them.

In the rest of this section, we describe an *abstract* global search theory that captures the essence of all (optimizing) global search algorithms. Every concrete search idea, such as the one discussed above, can then be formalized as a specialization of the abstract theory via a theory morphism. Two such specializations are used in Section 5.

Sorts $D, R, \hat{R}, C$
Operations
  $I : D \rightarrow Bool$
  $O : D \times R \rightarrow Bool$
  $\hat{I} : D \times \hat{R} \rightarrow Bool$
  $\hat{r}_0 : D \rightarrow \hat{R}$
  $Satisfies : R \times \hat{R} \rightarrow Bool$
  $Split : D \times \hat{R} \times \hat{R} \rightarrow Bool$
  $Extract : R \times \hat{R} \rightarrow Bool$
  $c : R \rightarrow C$
  $\leq : C \times C \rightarrow Bool$
Axioms
  GS0. $I(x) \implies \hat{I}(x, \hat{r}_0(x))$
  GS1. $I(x) \wedge \hat{I}(x, \hat{r}) \wedge Split(x, \hat{r}, \hat{s}) \implies \hat{I}(x, \hat{s})$
  GS2. $I(x) \wedge O(x, z) \implies Satisfies(z, \hat{r}_0(x))$
  GS3. $I(x) \wedge \hat{I}(x, \hat{r}) \implies$
  $Satisfies(z, \hat{r}) = (\exists \hat{s}.\ Split^*(x, \hat{r}, \hat{s}) \wedge Extract(z, \hat{s}))$
  GSC. $\leq$ is total ordering on C

Figure 4. Abstract global search theory.

The abstract global search theory is shown in figure 4. It is an extension of the problem specification $\langle D, R, I, O \rangle$. The new sort $\hat{R}$ is the type of search space descriptors. The predicate $\hat{I}$ characterizes *legal* search space descriptors. In the example above, $\hat{I}$ contains the condition that S and T form a partition of U. For an input $x : D$, $\hat{r}_0(x)$ is the initial search space. Axiom **GS0** ensures that the initial search space is legal.

The descendent relation on legal search spaces is given by *Split*. $Split(x, \hat{r}, \hat{s})$ is true if $\hat{s}$ is a (direct) subspace of $\hat{r}$ for an input x. By axiom **GS1**, all children of a legal subspace are again legal. The solutions that are obtainable from a single node $\hat{r}$ of the search tree are described by $Extract(z, \hat{r})$.

By axiom **GS3**, $Satisfies(z, \hat{r})$ describes the solutions z contained in a search space $\hat{r}$ that can be found with finite effort. We assume that x is a valid input, $I(x)$, and $\hat{r}$ is a legal descriptor for x $\hat{I}(x, \hat{r})$. Then $Satisfies(z, \hat{r})$ means that there exists a search space $\hat{s}$ from which we can extract z and that is connected to $\hat{r}$ by a *finite* path in the search tree. The latter condition is expressed by $Split^*$ which is defined in the following way.

$$Split^*(x, \hat{r}, \hat{s}) = (\exists k : nat.\ Split^k(x, \hat{r}, \hat{s}))$$
$$Split^0(x, \hat{r}, \hat{s}) = (\hat{r} = \hat{s})$$
$$Split^{k+1}(x, \hat{r}, \hat{s}) = (\exists \hat{t}.\ Split(x, \hat{r}, \hat{t}) \wedge Split^k(x, \hat{t}, \hat{s}))$$

Since we wish to find a *globally* optimal solution, **GS2** requires that all feasible solutions z for a valid input x are contained in the initial search space $\hat{r}_0(x)$.

Finally, the sort C is the range of the cost function c. By axiom **GSC**, it is totally ordered with respect to the ordering relation $\leq$. Thus, it makes sense to define an optimal solution z as one with minimal cost $c(z)$.

> **Function** $F(x : D)$
>   **where** $I(x)$
>   **returns** $(z: R \mid min(c, z, \{z' \mid O(x, z')\}))$
> $= f\_gs(x, \hat{r}_0(x))$
>
> **Function** $f\_gs(x : D, \hat{r} : \hat{R})$
>   **where** $I(x) \wedge \hat{I}(x, \hat{r}) \wedge \Phi(x, \hat{r})$
>   **returns** $(z : R \mid min(c, z, \{z' \mid Satisfies(z', \hat{r}) \wedge O(x, z')\}))$
> $= \textbf{some} \ (z : R \mid min(c, z, \{z' \mid Extract(z, \hat{r}) \wedge O(x, z')\}$
> $\cup \{f\_gs(x, \hat{s}) \mid Split(x, \hat{r}, \hat{s}) \wedge \Phi(x, \hat{s})\}))$

Figure 5.   Global search algorithm schema.

Based on the theory of figure 4, we can provide a schematic algorithm F that computes, for an input x with $I(x)$, a minimum cost solution z for which $O(x, z)$ holds. This algorithm is shown in figure 5. The function f_gs implements the actual search and is called by F with the initial search space $\hat{r}_0(x)$. It returns some z with minimal cost that is either directly extracted from the parameter search space $\hat{r}$, i.e. it is an element of $\{z' \mid Extract(z, \hat{r}) \wedge O(x, z')\}$, or that is obtained by splitting $\hat{r}$ and recursively applying f_gs to its subspaces $\hat{s}$.

In addition to the elements of the abstract global search theory, this algorithm uses a *necessary filter* Φ to prune branches of the search tree. Necessary filters are defined by the implication

$$I(x) \wedge \hat{I}(x, \hat{r}) \wedge (\exists z : R. \ Satisfies(z, \hat{r}) \wedge O(x, z)) \implies \Phi(x, \hat{r}) \tag{4}$$

This means if $\Phi(x, \hat{r})$ does *not* hold then there are no feasible solutions in $\hat{r}$ and we need not search this space.

Note that the theory of figure 4 does not guarantee termination of F. Infinite chains of split operations are possible as well as infinitely many subspaces of a search space. Furthermore, totality of F on valid inputs is not ensured because the global search theory does not require feasible solutions to exist for all valid inputs, i.e. it does not entail

$$\forall x : D. \ I(x) \implies \exists z : R. \ O(x, z)$$

3.2. *Algorithm design*

How can we find a global search algorithm for a given problem specification? We have to find a search space description $\hat{R}$ and operations $\hat{r}_0$, *Satisfies*, *Split*, and *Extract* such that the global search axioms are fulfilled.

In the KIDS approach this is done by referring to knowledge about search strategies on concrete data structures that is formalized in a library of general global search theories. We used Appendix A of (Smith, 1987) in our case study. Examples are theories to enumerate all sequences over a finite set and to enumerate all mappings between finite sets. A global search theory for a given problem is constructed by specializing a theory from

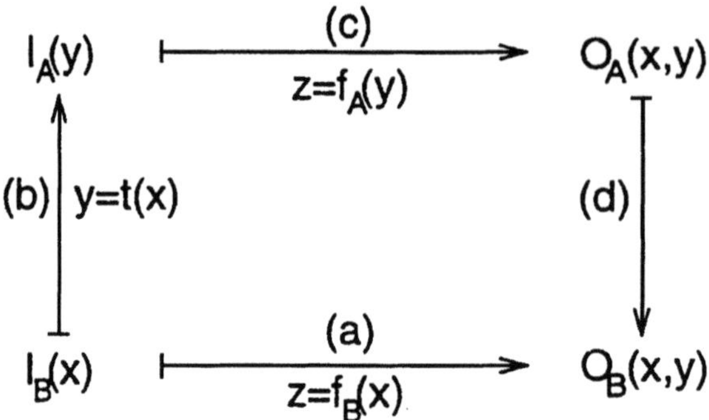

Figure 6.   Specialization.

the library. A problem theory $\mathcal{A} = \langle D_A, R_A, I_A, O_A \rangle$ *specializes* to a problem theory $\mathcal{B} = \langle D_B, R_B, I_B, O_B \rangle$ if

$$\begin{aligned}
&R_B \subseteq R_A \\
&\wedge\, \forall x : D_B.\, \exists y : D_A.\, \forall z : R_B. \\
&\quad (I_B(x) \implies I_A(y)) \\
&\quad \wedge\, (I_B(x) \wedge O_B(x, z) \implies O_A(y, z))
\end{aligned} \tag{5}$$

Condition (5) basically says that every solution z for $\mathcal{B}$ is also a solution for $\mathcal{A}$. Thus, if we know how to construct solutions for $\mathcal{A}$ and we can easily decide if a solution for $\mathcal{A}$ also is a solution for $\mathcal{B}$, then we have found a way to construct solutions for $\mathcal{B}$. Figure 6 further illustrates this idea. We want to construct an algorithm f_B for this problem, i.e. we want to implement transition (a) at the bottom of figure 6. Suppose that we know a solution f_A for $\mathcal{A}$ which implements transition (c). If $\mathcal{A}$ specializes to $\mathcal{B}$ then we know that we can find an input y of f_A for every input x of $\mathcal{B}$. Application of f_A gives us an $\mathcal{A}$-solution z (c). The final step (d) is to test if z fulfills O_B. In this way, the problem of finding an algorithm for $\mathcal{B}$ reduces to finding corresponding inputs in step (b) and deciding if O_B holds in step (d).

Verifying (5) and finding the mapping t from $\mathcal{B}$-inputs to $\mathcal{A}$-inputs can be done hand in hand if we construct a witness for the existential quantification over y while proving (5). This witness, in general, is a term depending on x which can be interpreted as a function from D_B to D_A.

Global search theories are extensions of problem theories. If we find a global search theory in our library whose problem theory specializes to the problem $\mathcal{B}$ at hand, we can extend $\mathcal{B}$ to a global search theory using $\hat{r}_0$, *Satisfies*, etc. of the library theory where we substitute the witness $t(x)$ for the input parameters. How this exactly works is shown in Section 5.

In general, the algorithm obtained by instantiating the schema of figure 5 is very inefficient. But it has a high potential for optimization which can be exploited by deriving a choice of filters, by program transformation, and by data structure refinement. The optimizations we have applied in the case study are discussed in Section 6.

4. A process model

Our presentation of the application domain theory and problem specification in Section 2 only describes the final result of the specification effort. To develop the domain theory is one of the major tasks if not the most complex and time consuming one in the KIDS approach. Much of its complexity stems from two requirements we demand of the domain theory: it must not only make precise the informal—usually incomplete and sometimes inconsistent— ideas about the nature and context of the problem, but it must also be formulated so as to aid and not impede the subsequent design process. The KIDS approach does not provide direct help to construct domain theories. In contrast, it needs a formal domain theory to work on and can smoothly be applied only if the presentation of this theory has a suitable syntactic form.

As a consequence, it is very unlikely that a satisfactory domain theory can be built from scratch. This observation led us to integrate the KIDS approach with the prototyping and spiral models of software engineering (Boehm, 1988). One cycle of development, as sketched in figure 7, has three phases. The first is concerned with establishing or enhancing the domain theory, the second produces code, and in the third phase code and theory are tested and validated.

We found it useful to build the first draft of the domain theory in parallel with a prototype. In this early phase, shaded gray in figure 7, the domain theory is not rich enough to apply algorithm design knowledge from design theories. Building a prototype enables us to get

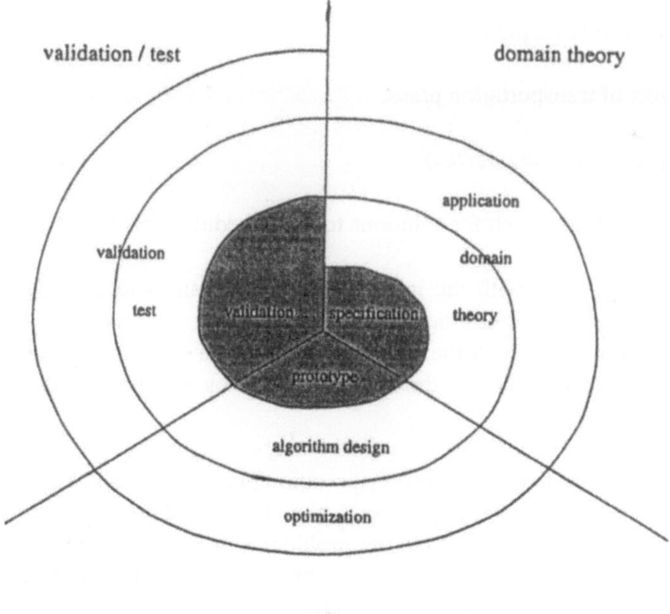

Figure 7. Process model.

a deeper understanding of the problem and the essential properties of the application area. It helps us to build a complete domain theory and to avoid dead-end developments.

The way in which the domain model is expressed, the data structures used, and the properties stated, can have much influence on the ease with which algorithm design can be carried out. Thus, what seems to be one cycle of design in figure 7, may in practice require several rounds of refining the domain theory until the formalized notions smoothly fit with the design theory we wish to use. This situation seems to be typical for *constructive* formal methods like program synthesis and transformation or interactive mechanical theorem proving. The more we wish to systematically construct solutions and provide tool support for this process, the more important becomes the syntactic presentation of our problems.

One example from the baggage transportation case study is the way we modeled delays in routes (cf. Section 2.2). In an early version of the domain theory, we described them by repetitions of the input nodes in paths, each occurrence of the input node denoting a delay of one time unit. This forced us to introduce predicates to characterize legal routes, and we could not use an acyclic graph model. When we decided to reformulate the theory and make delays explicit the theory became much more elegant and further design was much easier.

The process of theory refinement perpetuates as we derive filters and optimize code. The validation and test phases also serve us to validate the code with respect to properties, that are not captured by the design knowledge put to our disposal in the KIDS approach. Examples for such properties are the adequacy of domain theories and the efficiency of the synthesized code.

5. Two ways to find transportation plans

Looking at the sort of transportation plans,

$$map(baggage, nat \times seq(vertex))$$

suggests two strategies to search for solutions to our scheduling problem.

1. *Domain extension.* Start with the initially empty map and successively extend it by assigning possibly delayed feasible paths to baggage.
2. *Image modification.* Start with the map that assigns their source nodes and no delay to all baggage; successively modify the assigned routes by extending paths or increasing delays.

Both strategies enumerate all feasible transportation plans. In the KIDS approach, search strategies are provided in a library of general global search theories. Algorithm design proceeds by specializing one of these to the problem at hand. The first condition in (5), $R_B \subseteq R_A$, suggests matching the output domains of the problem specification with the ones of the library theories to find candidates to specialize.

When we began algorithm design for the transportation problem, our initial idea was to use the image modification strategy, but there is no general global search theory documented in the KIDS library (Smith, 1987) that models image modification. Instead, we found a theory that describes domain extension. This motivated us to explore both approaches.

5.1. Domain extension

Searching Appendix A of (Smith, 1987), we found a global search theory that specializes to the transportation problem. The theory *gs_finite_mappings*. It is a generalization of the search strategy to enumerate finite mappings shown in figure 3 to arbitrary finite sets U and V. We present this theory by a theory morphism, mapping the signature of the abstract global search theory of figure 4 to concrete expressions.

$$F \mapsto \textit{gs\_finite\_mappings}$$
$$D \mapsto set(\alpha) \times set(\beta)$$
$$R \mapsto map(\alpha, \beta)$$
$$I \mapsto \lambda\langle U, V\rangle.\ |U| < \infty \wedge |V| < \infty$$
$$O \mapsto \lambda\langle U, V\rangle, N.\ N \in Map(U, V)$$
$$\hat{R} \mapsto set(\alpha) \times set(\alpha) \times map(\alpha, \beta)$$
$$\hat{I} \mapsto \lambda\langle U, V\rangle, \langle S, T, M\rangle.\ S \uplus T = U \wedge M \in Map(S, V)$$
$$\textit{Satisfies} \mapsto \lambda N, \langle S, T, M\rangle.(\forall x \in S.N(x) = M(x))$$
$$\hat{r}_0 \mapsto \lambda\langle U, V\rangle.\ \langle\{\}, U, \{\!\}\rangle$$
$$\textit{Split} \mapsto \lambda\langle U, V\rangle, \langle S, T, M\rangle, \langle S', T', M'\rangle.$$
$$(\exists a, b.\ a = arb(T) \wedge b \in V$$
$$\wedge \langle S', T', M'\rangle = \langle S + a, T - a, M \oplus \{a \mapsto b\}\rangle)$$
$$\textit{Extract} \mapsto \lambda N, \langle S, T, M\rangle.\ T = \{\} \wedge N = M$$

The first part of the morphism determines the problem theory. The input domain D is a pair of sets over arbitrary types α and β. The input condition I restricts the valid inputs $U: set(\alpha)$ and $V: set(\beta)$ to finite sets. The output range R consists of all finite mappings from α to β. Feasible outputs are characterized by the output condition O: the resulting mapping N must have domain U and range V. Formally the function *Map* is defined by

$$M \in Map(U, V) \Longleftrightarrow dom(M) = U \wedge \forall b \in dom(M).\ M(b) \in V \tag{6}$$

Note the difference between the sort $map(\alpha, \beta)$ and the term $Map(U, V)$: the latter denotes the set of all total mappings from U to V, and each of them has the sort $map(\alpha, \beta)$.

The rest of the morphism extends the problem theory to a global search theory. Search spaces $\hat{R}$ are denoted by triples where the first two components are sets over α and the last is a mapping from α to β. By $\hat{I}$, a particular search space is valid for inputs U and V only if S and T partition U, i.e. $S \uplus T = U$, and M is a total mapping from S to V.

When is a solution N contained in a (valid) search space $\langle S, T, M\rangle$, i.e. when does $\textit{Satisfies}(N, \langle S, T, M\rangle)$ hold? According to the idea of domain extension, M as it is determined so far must be compatible with N. This is true if the images of N and M are identical on S, which is the domain of M.

As discussed in Section 3.1, we get a direct subspace of $\langle S, T, M \rangle$ if we extend the domain of M by exactly one element. This means we determine an arbitrary element $a = arb(T)$ of T and some value b of V, and extend M by mapping a to b, $M \oplus \{a \mapsto b\}$. To obtain a valid search space, we move a from T into S. Finally, if T is empty we have found a total mapping from U to V which we can extract.

In order to use *gs_finite_mappings* to construct an algorithm for the transportation problem, we have to show that its problem specification specializes to (3). The first step (cf. the specialization condition (5)) is to ensure that the range sort of the transportation problem is a subsort of the range sort of *gs_finite_mappings*. Unifying the two sort expressions, we find substitutions for the type variables in *gs_finite_mappings*.

$$\alpha \mapsto baggage$$

$$\beta \mapsto route$$

With this substitution, we get an instance of *gs_finite_mappings* whose output domain is equal to the one of *transport_plan*. It remains to find expressions in g and bs for U and V so that we can prove the specialization condition relating the two theories.

$$\forall \langle g, bs \rangle.\ \exists \langle U, V \rangle.\ \forall M.$$
$$(acyclic(g) \wedge \forall b \in bs.\ \exists p.\ feasible\_path(g, b, p) \implies |U| < \infty \wedge |V| < \infty)$$
$$\wedge\ (acyclic(g) \wedge \forall b \in bs.\ \exists p.\ feasible\_path(g, b, p)$$
$$\wedge\ \forall b \in dom(M).\ feasible\_path(g, b, snd(M(b)))$$
$$\wedge\ bs = dom(M) \wedge capacity\_bounded(g, M)$$
$$\implies M \in Map(U, V)) \tag{7}$$

The last implication gives the clue to find expressions for U and V. If we compare the definition of *Map* with the premise of the implication, we find two matching conjuncts. First, $dom(M) = U$ matches $bs = dom(M)$ if we substitute bs for U. Second, $\forall b \in dom(M).\ M(b) \in V$ and $\forall b \in dom(M).\ feasible\_path(g, b, snd(M(b)))$ are similar. Regarding predicates as propositions of membership of their extensions

$$P(x) \iff x \in \{y \mid P(y)\}$$

suggests to use the set of all feasible paths as a substitution for V. Unfortunately, *feasible_path* depends on a particular bag b, while V must contain candidate routes for all members of bs. Analyzing the situation might suggest to use

$$\{\langle n, p \rangle \mid \exists b \in bs.\ feasible\_path(g, b, p)\}$$

as a substitution for V because quantification is the only way to "hide" b in the expression for V. Only to consider paths that are feasible for *all* bags of bs is certainly not useful—this set typically is empty because there are bags with different sources or destinations. This analysis appears rather complex and there is a much simpler way to come to a substitution for

V: expanding the definition (1) of *feasible_path*, we find that only the conjunct *is_path*(g, p) does not depend on b. The remaining conditions for feasible paths are naturally exploited by developing a necessary filter, as we show at the end of the section.

Still, just to take the set of all paths in g is not restrictive enough to make V a *finite* set because it does not restrict the delay n of the routes in V. We therefore introduce an upper bound $md(g, bs)$ on delays, and define the set of all routes through g with a delay less than or equal to $md(g, bs)$ by

$$routes(g, bs) = \{\langle n, p\rangle \mid is\_path(g, p) \wedge n \leq md(g, bs)\}$$

With this definition, we finally come to use the sets

$$U \mapsto bs$$
$$V \mapsto routes(g, bs)$$

to specialize *gs_finite_mappings*.

Since there are feasible paths for all bags in bs (cf. the precondition of *transport_plan* in (3)), we can assign to $md\,(g, bs)$ the sum of the times needed to traverse a feasible path for each bag. Applying the substitution for α, β, U and V to *gs_finite_mappings* gives us a global search theory for *transport_plan*.

$$\hat{R} \mapsto set(baggage) \times set(baggage) \times plan$$
$$\hat{I} \mapsto \lambda\langle g, bs\rangle, \langle S, T, M\rangle.\ S \uplus T = bs$$
$$\wedge\ M \in Map(bs, routes(g, bs))$$
$$Satisfies \mapsto \lambda N, \langle S, T, M\rangle.\ \forall b \in S.\ N(b) = M(b))$$
$$\hat{r}_0 \mapsto \lambda\langle g, bs\rangle.\ \langle\{\}, bs, \{\!\{\,\}\!\}\rangle$$
$$Split \mapsto \lambda\langle g, bs\rangle, \langle S, T, M\rangle, \langle S', T', M'\rangle.$$
$$(\exists b, r.\ b = arb(T)$$
$$\wedge\ r \in routes(g, bs)$$
$$\wedge\ \langle S', T', M'\rangle = \langle S + b, T - b, M \oplus \{\!\{b \mapsto r\}\!\}\rangle)$$
$$Extract \mapsto \lambda N, \langle S, T, M\rangle.\ T = \{\} \wedge N = M$$

Note that "substituting" for U and V, which are bound variables, here means to apply the components of *gs_finite_mappings* to the pair of values for U and V and then abstracting over the input parameters of *transport_plan*.

Also note that the global search theory for *transport_plan* contains the problem (3) rather than the problem specification of *gs_finite_mappings*. In this way, the more restrictive pre- and postconditions are incorporated into the search algorithm when we instantiate the schema of figure 5.

The resulting search strategy assigns complete routes to one bag after the other. Without further optimization, *Split* assigns arbitrary routes to bags, and only when a complete plan can be extracted it is tested whether the assigned routes are feasible. An obvious way to prevent infeasible assignments in the first place is to develop a necessary filter. Actualization of (4), and the fact that *capacity_bounded* is monotonic in domain extensions of M gives us

$$\Phi \mapsto \lambda\langle g, bs\rangle, \langle S, T, M\rangle.$$
$$(\forall b \in S.\ source\ (b) = fst(snd(M(b)))$$
$$\wedge\ dest\ (b) = last(snd(M(b)))$$
$$\wedge\ path\_can\_carry(g, p, snd(M(b))))$$
$$\wedge\ capacity\_bounded(g, M)$$

Here, we have found an easy way to incorporate the remaining conjuncts of *feasible_path* into the algorithm.

5.2. *Image modification*

There is no global search theory documented in (Pressburger et al., 1991; Smith, 1987; Smith, 1990) that supports searching for maps by image modification. So we developed a new theory for this purpose.[1]

Abstracting from the concrete scheduling problem, the image modification strategy can be sketched as follows: The images of a given map (the initial schedule) are increased along the various degrees of freedom that are given by the range type of the map. A suitable successor relation on the elements of the range type can be used to describe the "direction" in which to increase the images of the map. This idea is formalized in *gs_parallel_mappings*.

$$F \mapsto gs\_parallel\_mappings$$
$$D \mapsto map(\alpha, \beta) \times set(\beta \times \beta)$$
$$R \mapsto map(\alpha, \beta)$$
$$I \mapsto \lambda\langle M, S\rangle.$$
$$|dom(M)| < \infty \wedge \forall x.\ \neg(x\ S\ x)$$
$$\wedge\ (\forall x, y.\ x\ S\ y \implies \neg(\exists z.\ x\ S\ z \wedge z\ S\ y))$$
$$O \mapsto \lambda\langle M, S\rangle, N.$$
$$dom(M) = dom(N)\ \wedge$$
$$\forall x \in dom(M).\ M(x)\ S^* N(x)$$
$$\hat{R} \mapsto map(\alpha, \beta) \times set(\beta \times \beta)$$
$$\hat{I} \mapsto \lambda\langle M, S\rangle, \langle M', S'\rangle.$$
$$S = S'\ \wedge\ dom(M) = dom(M')$$
$$\wedge\ \forall x \in dom(M).\ M(x)\ S^* M'(x)$$
$$Satisfies \mapsto \lambda N, \langle M, S\rangle.\ (\forall x \in dom(M).\ M(x)\ S^* N(x))$$
$$\hat{r}_0 \mapsto \lambda\langle M, S\rangle.\ \langle M, S\rangle$$
$$Split \mapsto \lambda\langle M, S\rangle, \langle M', S'\rangle, \langle M'', S''\rangle.$$
$$(\exists x, y.\ x = arb(dom(M')) \wedge M'(x)\ S\ y$$
$$\wedge\ \langle M'', S''\rangle = \langle M' \oplus \{x \mapsto y\}, S\rangle)$$
$$Extract \mapsto \lambda N, \langle M, S\rangle.\ N = M$$

The inputs are a map M and a binary relation S on the range of M. We model the relation by a set of pairs. The input condition I requires that the domain of M is finite and that S is irreflexive and non-dense. We use $x\, S\, y$ as a notation for $\langle x, y \rangle \in S$ to increase readability. Non-density means that there is no z "between" any two values x and y with $x\, S\, y$. This is necessary to ensure that all solutions can be found by finitely many applications of *Split*. Since we just want to modify the image of input M, a solution N is a mapping with the same domain as M. Furthermore, each image $N(x)$ is reachable from the corresponding input image $M(x)$ by S, i.e. the pair $\langle M(x), N(x) \rangle$ lies in the reflexive and transitive closure S^* of S.

Search spaces of $\hat{R}$ are pairs of maps and relations. The invariant $\hat{I}$ and the initial search space $\hat{r}$—which is the identity function—tell us that the relation is always the input relation S. We must include S in search spaces because we have to refer to it in *Satisfies*: a solution N is contained in a search space with mapping M if the images of N are reachable from M by S^*. The remainder of $\hat{I}$ is the output condition $O(M, M')$ for the maps in the search spaces. This shows that—unlike with *gs_finite_mappings*—we can extract a solution from every search space, namely its first component.

To split a search space $\langle M', S' \rangle$, we choose an arbitrary element x of the domain of M' and a direct successor y of $M'(x)$ under S. The new map M'' is constructed by overriding the image of x under M' by y.

The theory *gs_parallel_mappings* is a very abstract formalization of the idea searching for a mapping by image modification. There are only few restrictions on the successor relation S which determines the way search is actually performed. We could only put more restrictions on S if we made assumptions on the particular structure of the range sort β. But the resulting theory would be more specialized than is necessary to capture the search idea. This would restrict the range of problems to which it could be applied and is therefore undesirable.

5.2.1. Data type driven specialization.

Since we now have a theory that captures our search idea, we proceed by specializing the theory to the transportation problem as we did in Section 5.1. The instance of the specialization condition (5) reveals a drawback of the generality of *gs_parallel_mappings*.

$$
\begin{aligned}
&map(\alpha, \beta) \subseteq plan \\
&\wedge \\
&\forall \langle g, bs \rangle.\, \exists \langle M, S \rangle.\, \forall N. \\
&\quad (acyclic(g) \wedge \forall b \in bs.\, \exists p.\, feasible\_path\,(g, b, p) \\
&\quad \implies \\
&\qquad (|dom(M)| < \infty \wedge \forall x.\, \neg(x\, S\, x) \\
&\qquad \wedge (\forall x, y.\, x\, S\, y \implies \neg(\exists z.\, x\, S\, z \wedge z\, S\, y)))) \\
&\wedge \\
&\quad (acyclic(g) \wedge \forall b \in bs.\, \exists p.\, feasible\_path\,(g, b, p) \\
&\quad \wedge \forall b \in dom(N).\, feasible\_path\,(g, b, snd(N(b))) \\
&\quad \wedge bs = dom(N) \\
&\quad \wedge capacity\_bounded(g, N) \\
&\qquad \implies dom(M) = dom(N) \\
&\qquad \wedge (\forall x \in dom(M).\, M(x)\, S^*\, N(x)))
\end{aligned}
\tag{8}
$$

This condition does not help much in systematically finding a substitution for M and S. Since *gs_parallal_mappings* does not make assumptions on the structure of β, comparing the syntactic structure of the input/output conditions of the global search theory and the transportation problem does not provide candidates for S and M.

At this point of the development, we could appeal to human intuition, invent substitutions for S and M, and verify that they are witnesses for (8). But this would contradict the general KIDS approach of systematically constructing unknowns wherever possible. Instead, we propose to specialize *gs_parallel_mappings* in two steps. The first step determines a suitable successor relation S while the second step finds a substitution for M.

To determine S, we first analyze the condition $map(\alpha, \beta) \subseteq plan$ to find substitutions for the type variables α and β. Unification of the two sorts yields

$$\alpha \mapsto baggage$$
$$\beta \mapsto nat \times seq(vertex)$$

Now we can analyze the range type $nat \times seq(vertex)$ to find a successor relation on its elements based the basic types it is composed of. We know the usual successor function on natural numbers, and a canonical way to extend sequences is to append an element. In analogy to lexicographical orderings on pairs, we construct a successor relation by extending either element of a pair. Thus, we define S by

$$\langle n, p \rangle \ S \ \langle m, q \rangle \iff (n + 1 = m \wedge p = q) \vee (n = m \wedge (\exists v.\ p \ \langle v \rangle = q)) \tag{9}$$

This definition fulfills the conditions on S in (8), namely irreflexivity and non-denseness. For the reflexive and transitive closure of S we get

$$\langle n, p \rangle \ S^* \ \langle m, q \rangle \iff (n \leq m) \vee (\exists y.\ p ++ y = q) \tag{10}$$

With this definition for S^* it remains to show

$$
\begin{aligned}
&\forall \langle g, bs \rangle.\ \exists M.\ \forall N. \\
&(acyclic(g) \wedge \forall b \in bs.\ \exists p.\ feasible\_path(g, b, p) \implies |dom(M)| < \infty) \\
&\wedge \\
&(acyclic(g) \wedge \forall b \in bs.\ \exists p.\ feasible\_path(g, b, p) \\
&\wedge \forall b \in dom(N).\ feasible\_path(g, b, snd\ (N(b))) \\
&\wedge bs = dom(N) \\
&\wedge capacity\_bounded(g, N) \\
&\implies dom(M) = dom(N) \\
&\qquad \wedge (\forall x \in dom(M).\ (fst(M(x)) \leq fst(N(x)) \\
&\qquad \wedge (\exists q.\ snd(M(x))\ q = snd(N(x))))))
\end{aligned} \tag{11}
$$

As in Section 5.1, we can now easily determine a substitution for M. It assigns to each b in bs the non-delayed path only consisting of the source node of b.

$$M \mapsto \{b \mapsto \langle 0, \langle source(b) \rangle \rangle \mid b \in bs\}$$

With this information, we can finally set up the image modification theory for the transportation problem like we did in Section 5.1.

6.   Optimization and results

The algorithms resulting from the instantiation of the schema in figure 5 are well structured but very inefficient. Optimization of these algorithms is mandatory. Three classes of optimizations suggest themselves: filter development, program transformations, and refinement of data structures. The implemented system KIDS supports program transformations such as finite differencing and case distinction. It also supports developing necessary filters. In (Smith, 1987), various notions of filters for global search algorithms are formalized, and it is suggested to implement search heuristics by using priority queues to store search space descriptors.

Performing program transformations and data structure refinements on a formal basis is very costly and nearly impossible without machine support. We therefore decided to use the above optimization techniques as guidelines for our implementation but to build the implementation in an "ad-hoc" way without using formal techniques. We chose the functional programming language ML for the final implementation because functional programming offers an easy way to express instances of the program schema of figures in a programming language.

The strongest necessary filter which we have found for the algorithm of Section 5.1 is based on *capacity_bounded*: only partial plans which do not exceed the transportation capacity of any belt can be extended to complete, feasible plans. A stronger filter deciding if delaying a path can lead to a solution would be desirable, but without further assumptions on the transportation net such a filter is not obvious.

When we split a search space the test on *capacity_bounded* for the extended plan need only inspect the belts that are contained in the newly added route. This optimization can be regarded as an application of the "case distinction" transformation.

For the algorithm of Section 5.2 the situation is more complicated: the predicate *capacity_bounded* is not monotonic in increasing delays and can therefore not serve as a necessary filter. According to the successor relation S defined in (9), *Split* increases delays by one to generate direct subspaces. If *capacity_bounded* does not hold for the generated plan it may nevertheless hold for plans where the delay is increased by more than one unit. Consequently, we optimize *Split* and generate plans with minimally increased delays such that *capacity_bounded* holds.

Both algorithms need information that can be computed from the input once and for all, e.g. the feasible paths for all bags depend only on the input transportation net and not on search spaces. This information is precomputed before starting the search, which is an example application of finite differencing.

As suggested in (Smith, 1987), we use a priority queue to store search spaces. Crucial for efficiency is the choice of an ordering for the queue. The cost of the partial plans obviously has highest priority, but the classes of plans with equal costs are large and a finer ordering is needed. We have implemented the heuristic of searching "more complete" spaces first. For the domain extension algorithm, plans with larger domains have priority, while for

Table 1.   Size of theories and programs.

Document	Lines
Library of basic data structure specifications	490
Domain theory	240
Algorithm theory	350
ML implementation code	970

the image modification algorithm, we prefer plans with longer paths and smaller total delays.

Finally, it turns out that the implementation of basic data structures like mappings and sets also has a great effect on the total performance. It is tempting to closely stay with the abstract data structures used in algorithm design and use a library of implementations for maps and sets. Implementing sets and tuples by lists, and using so-called *splay dicts* of the Standard ML library to implement maps, however, significantly increased performance.

In spite of these optimizations, performance of both algorithms is still poor, and only small examples can be treated in reasonable time. The major obstacle to better performance is that resolving conflicts by delays results in an extremely high branching factor of the search tree.

Test runs show that the image modification algorithm is in general faster than the domain extension algorithm. The difference in performance increases with the branching degree of the transportation net. We believe this justifies the extra effort needed to develop the global search theory of Section 5.2.

The size of theories and programs are summarized in Table 1.

Approximately half of the ML code implements the data structures for the transportation net, while the rest implements the actual scheduling algorithms. The code is well-structured and highly reusable. Both algorithms share most of the code which facilitates exploring alternatives.

The case study required an effort of approximately 9 person months. We spent about one third of that time to learn the KIDS approach. Approximately 75% of the remaining time was devoted to building the domain theory.

7.   Related work

Approaches to algorithm design and program synthesis roughly fall in two categories. The ones advocating a calculational style of program development like the Dijkstra/Gries method (Gries, 1981), the refinement calculus (Morgan, 1990) or Dershowitz's approach (Dershowitz, 1983) are tuned towards application by hand. Others like deductive program synthesis (Bibel, 1980; Hanna and Waldinger, 1980), program construction based on type-theory (Constable et al., 1986) and the approaches introduced in (Lowry and McCartney, 1991) focus on machine-supportable techniques. However, most of them, mechanized or not, are oriented on the syntactical structure of logical formulas or programming language constructs. They provide rules, e.g. to construct loops, or they describe how to synthesize programs, e.g. from specifications with conjunctive postconditions.

The KIDS approach differs from these in that it provides design steps reflecting *significant* design decisions. Algorithm theories abstract from implementation details for a particular programming language and characterize classes of algorithms (not programs) by logical theories. To achieve the effect of a design step like global search for a particular problem, many rule applications would be needed in other calculi, and—more important—these steps would have to re-invent the principles of search algorithms. The proof obligations arising would incorporate correctness conditions of global search—intertwined with conditions on the particular application domain and the specific code produced. Abstracting from these details, KIDS separates algorithm design from optimization concerns, and makes design knowledge amenable to re-use not on the level of code but on the conceptual level.

There are several attempts to improve confidence in the correctness of the synthesized algorithms by mechanically verifying the underlying theory. Kreitz (1993) has formalized global search in the Nuprl type theory (Constable et al., 1986). He specifically addresses the problem of termination and prevents infinite branchings of the search tree by using only finite sets in his formalization. He introduces *wf-filters* to prune infinite branches and proposes to provide a collection of wf-filters for each theory.

The value of mechanical verification of design theories and program transformations is much reduced if the relation between tools supporting the design process and the underlying theories is not clear. The approach to build transformation systems presented in (Kolyang et al., 1996) uses a generic theorem prover as the kernel of such a system. The prover is used to verify design theories and transformations as well as to support their application. This guarantees that the applied transformations are exactly the ones that have been verified. The approach is illustrated by proving and applying a global search theory on the basis of the generic theorem prover Isabelle (Paulson, 1994).

It seems to be unlikely to find "practically complete" knowledge bases for software construction systems. Such systems should be designed to ease routine extension of their knowledge bases so they can be adapted to specific application domains and grow with the users' experience. In (Heisel et al., 1995), a generic system architecture based on the notion of *strategies* is proposed. Strategy modules have a clearly defined interface to the system kernel, so new ones can be integrated into the system in a routine way. The system Specware (Srinivas and Jüllis, 1995) under development at Kestrel also seems to allow for a modularized and easily extendible knowledge base.

Our case study relates to the research on design of transportation schedulers at Kestrel (Smith and Parra, 1993; Smith et al., 1995). They study schedulers that assign trips to resources like planes, ships, and trucks to meet movement requirements. In this setting, trips fully occupy resources for an interval of time, i.e. the load of a resource cannot be extended during a trip. Furthermore, a trip changes the availability of a resource: the destination of one trip becomes the source of the next one. In baggage transportation, however, load of resources can continually change as baggage flows through the net, but source and destination points of a resource remain fixed in time.

Another difference lies in the focus of our work. For several years, a highly specialized theory on transportation scheduling has been developed at Kestrel with the aim to produce extremely efficient schedulers. Recently, this has even led to a refinement of the abstract global search theory (Smith et al., 1995). The purpose of our case study, in contrast, has been to study in how far the KIDS approach as documented in the literature can support programmers who have no particular experience with the approach, to design algorithms for a non-trivial problem.

8. Discussion

We focus the discussion of our experience with KIDS on three questions: why use a formal approach instead of ordinary programming; what are the peculiarities introduced by formality; and what are the distinct advantages and disadvantages of KIDS?

8.1. Why use a formal approach at all?

It is hard to speculate about the results an experienced programmer might have produced who started with knowledge about the problem domain similar to ours when we began the case study. But we can point out where formality helped us in the case study. In the first circle of the process model of figure 7, we implemented a prototype in an "ad-hoc" way to gain experience with the problem domain and come up with a first formal specification. Given our poor understanding of the problem at that time, the prototype revealed many aspects we had not been aware of. Formulating a specification afterwards and trying to identify these aspects of the problem in the specification forced us to search for a suitable level of abstraction to reason about the problem domain.

Having a *formal* specification and proving properties about it in the subsequent development revealed problems like overlapping search spaces and non-termination that we might have missed by just testing an implementation. Furthermore, testing was possible only after considerable optimization because the execution times—and traces—of non-optimized algorithms for the transportation problem were overwhelmingly large.

Concerning errors in an optimized program, the question arises whether a bug stems from the design or from the optimization. We believe that, although an experienced programmer with the right intuition might have been able to solve these problems with the program as the only "formal" document, formality helps in finding errors early and identifying their sources.

A formal specification not only provides an unambiguous, abstract documentation and the possibility to prove correctness of code relative to the specification. With the KIDS approach, design *decisions*—to construct a global search algorithm, to use image modification, what optimizations to apply—and their justifications are precisely documented as well.

8.2. Peculiarities introduced by formality

Some of the following observations may apply to formal methods in general, while arguably in a stronger sense to the KIDS approach because it is constructive and poses stronger requirements on the documents it deals with than mere "formal notations" or verification-based approaches.

Due to their preciseness, the logical theories on which the approach is based provide good reference points for software engineers who wish to learn and use them. Still, the theory of global search algorithms is inherently complex and it takes considerable effort to get a working knowledge of its application that enables one to map a particular problem to its formal representation.

The approach requires the existence of a formal problem specification. It does not directly address the first phase of the development, before a sufficiently complete application domain theory is available, which may be the most complex part of the process. We found prototyping useful to understand the problem domain, but more elaborate techniques to guide theory development remain to be established.

Moreover, the design theory one wants to apply later also influences theory development: the domain theory must supply the "right" notions and must be syntactically structured in a way that matches the design theory. For instance, defining plans as mappings from baggage to routes helps to apply the finite mappings design theory because of the similar type structure.

If the syntactic difference between the domain and design theories is too large, the constructive approach may be difficult to follow even if the domain theory semantically captures all necessary requirements. Several component predicates and properties of *feasible_path* defined in our domain theory serve to establish a terminology to adequately formulate instances of the global search axioms. These predicates strongly depend on the way *Split* is axiomatized. Thus a thorough understanding of the design theory is necessary to focus theory development.

Given a domain theory, the steps in designing a global search algorithm: specializing a theory, deriving filters, and applying optimizing program transformations, provide a clear separation of concerns. Specialization determines the basic structure of the search, necessary filters exploit properties of the application domain, and only the final program transformations and data type refinements eliminate redundancies in the code and "fuse" filters with the basic search structure to gain efficiency.

Each of these tasks corresponds to one cycle in the process model that we introduced in Section 4. Thus the model helps programmers to focus activities on a particular task and to avoid introducing certain design ideas at the "wrong" time into the development. In early attempts to design the algorithm of Section 5.2, we tried to introduce optimizations too early—trying to generate delayed routes only if necessary—which made our design much too complex.

8.3. *KIDS specific issues*

Let us review our decision not to use the implemented system KIDS but to try and apply the underlying "approach" manually. Initially, this decision was motivated by the steep learning curve we expected a complex system like KIDS to have. We also wanted to make sure that we would be able to track down difficulties with the case study to their proper sources: peculiarities of the case study or problems inherent in the KIDS approach. If we had relied on the system, then we could not have ruled out problems stemming from the implementation being a research prototype, or from our lacking experience using the system. To do so, we would have had to reconstruct the workings of the system, basically doing what we actually did when applying the approach manually.

In retrospect, we believe this decision is justified. Although we lost the possibility to actually apply optimizing program transformations, for the main task, namely to work with the global search design theory, our decision proved advantageous. The entire development of the image modification algorithm in Section 5.2 would not have been possible if we had confined ourselves to the working system. The system does not have an open design, and introducing a new global search theory would have been impossible for us to do. Furthermore, we would have needed to modify the specialization procedure to use the new theory, which again is a major programming task. Both, the approach and the system lack support for constructing new algorithm theories and incorporate them into the working system. These non-trivial tasks deserve support if the approach shall be applied routinely, because for routine applications tool support is indispensable.

Our experience with the image modification algorithm shows that it is advisable to stick to the approach even if no design theory supporting a particular design idea is available. In this situation, it pays to develop a new design theory that describes the desired search strategy in an abstract way. In (Dick, 1994), we decided to construct the problem specific algorithm theory of Section 5.2 in one step and to manually verify it against the abstract global search theory. This decision was mainly due to lack of experience and increased the complexity of the task considerably. Moreover, it led to a less efficient algorithm.

A problem of a more technical nature is that termination of the constructed algorithms is not addressed by the global search theory we have used. This lead us to the somewhat unnatural introduction of the upper bound $md(g, bs)$ on delays (cf. Section 5.1). Termination of global search algorithms can be spoiled in two ways. There may be branches of the search tree with infinite length, or there may be nodes with infinitely many children. In (Smith, 1990), a well-founded ordering is introduced into the abstract global search theory to prevent infinite chains of *Split*-operations. There are reasons not to require termination of all global search theories—termination may be addressed only when a library theory is specialized—but we would appreciate a systematic way that relieves programmers of dealing with termination on-the-fly.

As many formal techniques, KIDS cannot deal explicitly with non-functional requirements such as efficiency and maintainability, but the formal theory of filters in (Smith, 1987) guides the search for possible optimizations. Since the approach is constructive, domain theories and code are well-structured and well-documented. This enhances requirements traceability and maintainability. Furthermore, with a domain theory at hand, the KIDS approach is well suited to construct prototypes in little time, and to explore alternative designs.

Finally, KIDS is one of the few approaches combining formality with the representation of software construction steps of considerable complexity. A library of algorithm theories makes standard design knowledge explicit and formally accessible. Application of design theories takes place at a much higher level of abstraction than with the language oriented rules many other formal program design calculi supply. We believe that, in correspondence with conceptual developments like design patterns and software architectures in software engineering in general, formal methods have to adapt larger patterns of reasoning and build a theory of software construction that allows reasoning at abstract, problem oriented levels. KIDS shows a step in this direction.

Acknowledgments

We would like to thank David Basin, Maritta Heisel and Burkhart Wolff for fruitfull discussions. David, Maritta, Klaus Didrich and Martin Simons provided comments on drafts of this paper. Thanks also to the reviewers' whose comments helped to improve the presentation.

Note

1. Note, that there is no easy way to extend the "library" of global search theories of the implemented system KIDS because it is hard-coded into the implementation. Hence, we could not have used the system to work with the theory on image modification decribed in Section 5.2.

References

Bibel, W. 1980. Syntax-directed, semantics-supported program synthesis. *Artificial Intelligence*, 14:243–261.

Boehm, B.W. 1988. A spiral model of software development and enhancement. *IEEE Computer*, 21(5):61–72.

Constable, R. et al. 1986. *Implementing Mathematics with the Nuprl Proof Development System*, Prentice Hall.

Dershowitz, N. 1983. *The Evolution of Programs*, Birkhäuser.

Dick, S. 1994. Eine Fallstudie zur Entwicklung korrekter Software: Steuerung einer Gepäckförderanlage. Master's thesis, Dept. of Computer Science, Technical University of Berlin.

Gries, D. 1981. *The Science of Programming*, Springer-Verlag.

Heisel, M., Santen, T., and Zimmermann, D. 1995. Tool support for formal software development: A generic architecture. In *Software Engineering—ESEC'95*, W. Schäfer and P. Botella (Eds.), LNCS 989, Springer Verlag, pp. 272–293.

Kolyang, Santen, T., and Wolff, B. 1996. Correct and user-friendly implementation of transformation systems. In *FME'96—Industrial Benefits and Advances in Formal Methods*, LNCS, Springer Verlag.

Kreitz, C. 1993. *Meta-Synthesis. Deriving Programs that Develop Programs*, Technische Hochschule Darmstadt.

Lowry, M. and McCartney, R.D. (Eds.) 1991. *Automating Software Design*, Menlo Park: AAAI Press.

Manna, Z. and Waldinger, R. 1980. A deductive approach to program synthesis. *ACM Transactions on Programming Languages and Systems*, 2:90–121.

Morgan, C. 1990. *Programming from Specifications*, Prentice Hall.

Paulson, L.C. 1994. *Isabelle—A Generic Theorem Prover*, LNCS 828, Springer Verlag.

Smith, D.R. and Lowry, M.R. 1989. Algorithm theories and design tactics. In *Proc. International Conference on Mathematics of Program Construction*, J. van de Snepscheut (Ed.), Lecture Notes in Computer Science 375, Springer Verlag, 379–398.

Smith, D.R. 1987. Structure and design of global search algorithms. Technical Report Kes.U.87.12, Kestrel Institute.

Smith, D.R. 1990. KIDS: A semiautomatic program development system. *IEEE Transactions on Software Engineering*, 16(9):1024–1043.

Smith, D.R. and Parra, E.A. 1993. Transformational approach to transportation scheduling. In *Proceedings of the Eighth Knowledge-Based Software Engineering Conference*, Chicago.

Smith, D.R., Parra, E.A., and Westfold, S.J. 1995. Synthesis of high-performance transportation schedulers. Technical Report KES.U.95.6, Kestrel Institute.

Srinivas, J.V. and Jüllig, J. 1995. Specware: Formal support for composing software. In *Proceedings of the Third Conference on Mathematics of Program Construction*.

Pressburger, T.T., Gilham, L., and Smith, D.R. 1991. *Kestrel Interactive Development System*, Version 1.0, Kestrel Institute.

Acknowledgements

We would like to thank David Saxon, Martin Weiser, and [illegible] who [illegible] the [illegible]. We [illegible] Dr. Allan Pinkus and Dr. [illegible] for [illegible].

Automated Software Engineering, 4, 33–51 (1997)
© 1997 Kluwer Academic Publishers, Boston.

Specification and Animation of a Bank Transfer using KIDS/VDM

YVES LEDRU   yves.ledru@imag.fr
Laboratoire Logiciels Systèmes Réseaux, IMAG, B.P. 53, F-38041 Grenoble cedex 9, FRANCE

Abstract. The development of formal specifications may benefit from prototyping activities. The production of an executable model for a given description helps bridging the gap between this specification and the corresponding reality. The KIDS/VDM system, based on the KIDS environment, provides these prototyping facilities for the model-based specification language of VDM. This paper illustrates its use in the specification of a bank transfer operation. The specification process starts from an abstract specification and details it by a series of refinements of either the control flow or the data structures. The case study shows how animation may be helpful at several stages of the process. It favours the dialog between the specifier and his customer and helps assessing the correspondence between the description and the actual problem. It also convinces the specifier of the validity of his refinements before he fulfills the necessary proof obligations.

Keywords: formal methods, prototyping, VDM, refinements, program synthesis

1. Introduction

Recent reports [6, 4] have shown that model-based formal methods like Z [22] or VDM [11] are becoming part of industrial practice for critical applications, especially at the specification stage. The specification languages associated with these methods are mainly mathematical notations to express the precise description of a given system.

A first generation of tools has been proposed to support these formalisms. It is based on the syntax and static semantics of these languages, and ensures the syntactical conformance of a given text to the definition of the formalism. But syntactical conformance to a mathematical notation does not guarantee the high quality of a specification, which is the expected benefit of these techniques. For example, the mathematical formula $x \geq 5 \wedge x < 1$ can not be verified by any x value. It corresponds thus to a specification that can not be fulfilled.

A formal method like VDM provides several techniques to check that a specification has interesting mathematical properties (invariant preservation and implementability). For example, it defines a necessary condition for the implementability of specifications. The application of these techniques allows one to produce a consistent piece of mathematics but does not address an important topic in the validation of specifications: does it correspond to some real world problem?

One way to get further convinced of this correspondence is to produce an executable model of the specification and to confront it with the real world, e.g. by demonstrating it to a customer. This may be achieved by using an executable specification language, which is not the case for VDM and Z. The pros and cons of executable specifications have already been debated, among others in [8, 14]. As far as VDM is concerned, several attempts have been performed towards executable specifications [7, 13]. Two strategies may be followed:

- to concentrate on a subset of executable constructs of the language. This turns the specification language into a programming language. It may lead the specifier to overlook the non-executable constructs of the specification language and to specify unnecessary details for executability concerns.

- to informally translate the specification into a programming language close to the specification language. This distinction between languages prevents overspecification, but the link between specification and prototype is only informal and errors may result from the translation process. Moreover, the production of two descriptions, the specification and its prototype, increases the cost of the development.

This latter approach may be improved by an adequate tool support which

- ensures the correspondence between specification and prototype;

- automatizes parts of the development.

KIDS/VDM provides such a solution for the production of prototypes from VDM specifications. It exploits two knowledge-based software engineering tools: the REFINE[1] language [21] and the KIDS system [20]. The goal of this paper is to illustrate the use of KIDS/VDM on a case study and show how these techniques may be helpful in the specification process. A more complete description of KIDS/VDM, its principles and limitations can be found in [16].

Section 2 presents the case study, introduces the VDM method and proposes a first specification. Section 3 features two refinements of the initial specification and shows the benefit of this tool support. Finally, section 4 draws the conclusions of this work.

2.   Abstract specification of a bank transfer

At the 16th International Conference on Software Engineering, several participants of the Workshop on Software Engineering and Artificial Intelligence were asked by M. Feather to work on examples taken from the "Barclay's Code of Business Banking"[2]. This document explains the general principles of the operation of this bank. The bank transfer example presented here is based on common knowledge about business banking, combined with several elements from that document. Its objective is to illustrate how a VDM developer could use his tools for this kind of specification activity. Another response to this problem has been proposed by Chung and his colleagues [5]: it focuses on non-functional requirements and the support of change.

2.1.   Reuse of an existing specification

A good starting point in specification is to reuse an existing description of a bank transfer. The following VDM specification is taken from the teaching notes of [11].

2.1.1. Types and state variables

A VDM specification describes an "abstract machine", i.e. global variables associated with operations. The definition of state variables starts with the introduction of types:

- $Acno$ (account number) is a simple natural number

$Acno = \mathbb{N}$

- $Acdata$ (account data) groups in a record the name of the owner of the account (own), the current balance (bal), i.e. the amount of money available, and the absolute value of the overdraft limit (od), i.e. the limit on the possible negative balance; an invariant on the type $Acdata$ constrains the balance to be greater than or equal to the overdraft.

$$Acdata\ ::\ own\ :\ char^*$$
$$bal\ :\ \mathbb{Z}$$
$$od\ :\ \mathbb{N}$$

inv $(mk\text{-}Acdata(own, bal, od)) \triangleq bal \geq -od$

Once types have been defined, the state variables are introduced. Here, the state of the specification is made up of a single global variable am (accounts map) that stores a map from account numbers to account data.

$$Bank\ ::\ am\ :\ Acno\ \xrightarrow{m}\ Acdata$$

2.1.2. Operations on the state

In VDM, each operation is defined in terms of a pair of predicates that specify its pre- and post-conditions. In this case study, operations include: creation of a new account, deletion of an account, modification of account data such as the owner or the overdraft limit, and operations on the amounts stored on the accounts. In this paper, we will concentrate on the transfer operation ($TRANSF$).

- It takes three arguments as input: fr_ac, the account which will be debited, to_ac, the account which will be credited, and a, the amount of money transferred. This last parameter is a natural number strictly greater than zero.

- The operation has read and write access to the global variable am.

- A pre-condition states that both accounts given as inputs must be in the domain of the am map, that they must be different, and that the balance and overdraft associated with fr_ac must allow the transfer to take place.

- The post-condition expresses the final values of the state variable after the execution of the operation. It states that am is overwritten by a new map which only modifies the balances of both accounts given as parameters.

$$TRANSF\ (fr\_ac\text{:}\ Acno,\ to\_ac\text{:}\ Acno,\ a\text{:}\ \mathbb{N}_1)$$

ext wr $am\ :\ Acno \xrightarrow{m} Acdata$

pre $fr\_ac \in$ **dom** $am \land to\_ac \in$ **dom** $am \land fr\_ac \neq to\_ac$
  $\land\ bal(am(fr\_ac))\text{-}a \geq \text{-}od(am(fr\_ac))$

post $am = \overleftarrow{am} \dagger \{fr\_ac \mapsto \mu(\overleftarrow{am}(fr\_ac), bal \mapsto bal(\overleftarrow{am}(fr\_ac))\text{-}a),$
          $to\_ac \mapsto \mu(\overleftarrow{am}(to\_ac), bal \mapsto bal(\overleftarrow{am}(to\_ac)) + a)\}$

Some VDM notations need further explanations.

- The "hook" symbol ($\overleftarrow{\ \ }$), used in the post-condition, denotes the initial value of the state variable.

- The overriding operator ($\dagger$) is a binary operator on maps which returns the union of the second map with the pairs of the first map which are outside its domain.

- The μ function takes two arguments: a record and an association of a record field with a value. It returns the value of its first argument where the specified field has been replaced by the given value.

In the proposed ISO VDM standard [1], the specification of the initial state is a component of the state specification. Here, we use a slightly different (but equivalent) approach where the initial state is specified as an operation. In this case study, the post-condition of $INIT$ specifies an initial state with three accounts. For example, account 1 is owned by John, has a positive balance of 25000 and an overdraft limit of 10000.

$$INIT$$

ext wr $am\ :\ Acno \xrightarrow{m} Acdata$

pre $true$

post $am = \{1 \mapsto mk\text{-}Acdata(\text{John}, 25000, 10000),$
          $2 \mapsto mk\text{-}Acdata(\text{Paul}, 0, 0),$
          $3 \mapsto mk\text{-}Acdata(\text{George}, 5000, 10000)\}$

2.1.3. Proof obligations

Once a VDM specification has been stated, it must be proved to fulfill several mathematical properties. First, the invariants and types must be preserved by the operations. Second, the operation must be implementable, i.e. there must exist a final state that satisfies the post-condition provided the pre-condition was satisfied.

In this case, implementability is easy to demonstrate since the post-conditions provide the new values of the state variable. The main point is to check that the invariant associated with type $Acdata$ is preserved by the operations, i.e. that the balance remains greater than the overdraft limit. This is obvious for $INIT$, since all balances are positive. As far as $TRANSF$ is concerned, this is guaranteed by the last conjunct of the pre-condition.

The careful examination of these proof obligations may be stated more formally. Several books [11, 3] provide the necessary detailed framework to do so. It may even be supported by a proof assistant [12]. Nevertheless, in practice, this proof activity is most often performed very informally.

Further validation of the specification may be carried out by cross-reading or inspections. But a specification like the one of *TRANSF* involves a mathematical jargon that may only be read (and understood) by a VDM expert. This process guarantees that the specification is a consistent piece of mathematics but does not assess that this mathematical model corresponds to the described reality.

2.1.4.   Validation of the specification

In order to achieve a high quality specification, this specification should be validated by a bank specialist, who will presumably be unable to read the mathematical text of the specification. A dialog must thus take place between him and the developer. One way to facilitate this dialog is to prototype the specification.

2.2.   KIDS/VDM

The original idea of KIDS/VDM [18, 16] is to exploit the similarities between the specification language of VDM and the executable language REFINE [21]. Both languages share the same data types and data structures (sets, sequences, maps) and REFINE provides a wide spectrum of control constructs (functional, declarative, imperative). Experiments have shown that a VDM specification can be informally transformed into a REFINE program [17].

The Kestrel Interactive Development System (KIDS) [20] supports the synthesis of RE-FINE programs from functional specifications, written in a language named REGROUP. This synthesis process corresponds to the application of design tactics (e.g. global search, divide and conquer), simplifications by a theorem prover, and code optimizations. Every synthesis step is performed under the control of the environment which guarantees the correctness of the code with respect to its specification.

KIDS/VDM exploits the capabilities of the KIDS environment to

- control and support the transformation of VDM specifications into REFINE code;

- help discharge proof obligations of the VDM specification [15].

This second feature will not be considered in this paper which focuses on the use of KIDS/VDM to animate specifications.

The original KIDS environment supports two major modes (Fig. 1):

- the *program development* mode includes tools for the synthesis of programs from specifications;

- the *theory development* mode proposes tools to help the expression of REGROUP specifications and the development of inference rules for the theorem prover.

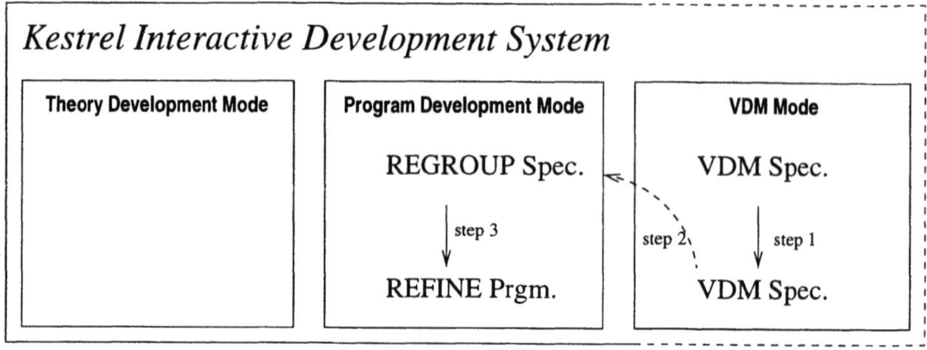

Figure 1. Prototyping a specification within KIDS/VDM

The KIDS/VDM environment adds a new mode to KIDS to support transformations of VDM specifications (Fig. 1). A typical development of a VDM specification goes through three main steps:

1. transformations of the original VDM specification, in the VDM mode; these transformations are automatic and rewrite several language constructs (e.g. subtyping) into a form closer to REGROUP;

2. translation of the resulting VDM specification into a combination of REGROUP specifications and REFINE programs;

3. synthesis of REFINE programs from these specifications, in the program development mode.

The principles of this process have already been detailed [18]. It is essentially automatic: interactions mainly occur in the KIDS development mode in order to select the design tactic or guide the optimization and simplification activities. Recent work on this system [16] has kept the underlying principles of the translation; it has increased the coverage of the VDM specification language, added design and proof knowledge in order to better support the kind of developments involved, and improved the automatization of the process.

In this case study, the following REFINE program has been automatically synthesized for *TRANSF*.

```
function TRANSF(FR-AC: integer, TO-AC: integer, A: integer)
               : any-type
= let(TRANSF-TUPLE: tuple(AM: map(integer, tuple(OWN: seq(char),
                                                 BAL: integer,
                                                 OD: integer)))
       = TRANSF-F(FR-AC, TO-AC, A, AM))
  AM <- TRANSF-TUPLE.1
```

It is a side-effecting function that modifies the AM variable by assigning to it the result of the TRANSF-F function. In the let construct, TRANSF-TUPLE is a tuple which is defined as the application of TRANSF-F to the input values of the function and the initial value of the global variables affected by the operation. Here AM is the only variable affected, so that the tuple is reduced to a single field.

TRANSF-F is a pure function that takes the initial value of state variable AM as an argument (named OLD-AM) and returns the new value of this variable. Its specification is automatically generated from the VDM specification. It is then transformed into the REFINE code listed below by the application of the KIDS tactic "spec-to-code". This tactic extracts the new value of AM from the equality in the post-condition. It also checks that several typing constraints are verified by the result: INV-NATURAL-4 and INV-NATURAL-1-4 respectively check that the account numbers and overdraft are natural values, INV-BAL-OD-2 checks that the typing invariant of *Acdata* is verified. A further KIDS optimization step has introduced the local variables C-1, C-2, and C-3 in order to avoid computing C-1 four times. C-1 is the actual result of the function: the corresponding let construct is the direct translation of the post-condition of the VDM *TRANSF* specification.

```
function TRANSF-F (FR-AC: integer, TO-AC: integer, A: integer,
                   OLD-AM: map(integer,tuple(OWN: seq(char),
                                     BAL: integer, OD: integer))
                 | ...)
returns
  (TRANSF-TUPLE: tuple(AM: map(integer,tuple(OWN: seq(char),
                                     BAL: integer, OD: integer)))
    | ... )
= let(C-3: tuple(OWN: seq(char), BAL: integer, OD: integer)
         = OLD-AM(TO-AC),
      C-2: tuple(OWN: seq(char), BAL: integer, OD: integer)
         = OLD-AM(FR-AC))
  let(C-1: map(any-type, any-type)
         = OVERRIDES(OLD-AM,
           {| FR-AC -> (let (var XXX: tuple(OWN: seq(char),
                             BAL: integer, OD: integer) = C-2)
                 XXX.BAL <- C-2.2 - A; XXX),
             TO-AC -> (let (var XXX: tuple(OWN: seq(char),
                             BAL: integer, OD: integer) = C-3)
                 XXX.BAL <- C-3.2 + A; XXX) |}))
  if INV-NATURAL-4(C-1) & INV-NATURAL-1-4(C-1) & INV-BAL-OD-2(C-1)
  then <C-1> else undefined
```

The REFINE language does not provide a map overriding operator. To support the translation of VDM specifications, it has thus been defined as a function in a general purpose KIDS theory:

```
function OVERRIDES(m1,m2): map (any-type,any-type)
```

```
= {| x -> (if defined?(m2(x)) then m2(x) else m1(x))
   |(x) x in (domain(m1) union domain(m2))|}
```

This definition only provides a way to compute map overriding, i.e. a map comprehension. In order to perform code simplifications, the theory should be complemented with axioms and theorems about this operator.

In summary, the synthesis of the prototype proceeds mainly automatically. The significant interactions with the environment are the choice of the spec-to-code tactic and the optimization of the resulting code. The resulting REFINE code has then been compiled into executable form.

The KIDS/VDM development may be carried on further in order to simplify the resulting program: in the context of the pre-condition, it may be proved that the guard of the `if ... then ... else` construct is always true and that the program may be simplified to `<C-1>`. Such a simplification not only speeds up the execution of the prototype, but also provides a proof of the implementability of the specification because `TRANSF-F` may no longer return `undefined`. Yet, performing this simplification is a proof process that may involve extensive user interaction.

2.3.   *Execution of the prototype*

2.3.1.   *A typical execution*

The execution of the prototype may give the following scenario:

- At the beginning, the *am* variable exists but its content is undefined.

  ```
  .> am
  RE:*UNDEFINED*
  ```

- The *INIT* operation is performed and the content of *am* is checked. Actually, since no output is specified for *INIT* or *TRANSF*, they return the new value of the state variable.

  ```
  .> (init)
  ((1 "John" 25000 10000) (2 "Paul" 0 0) (3 "George" 5000 10000))
  .> am
  ((1 "John" 25000 10000) (2 "Paul" 0 0) (3 "George" 5000 10000))
  ```

- A transfer of an amount of 1000 is executed between accounts 1 and 2. It may be checked that it modifies the accounts of John and Paul, and does not affect other accounts.

  ```
  .> (transf 1 2 1000)
  ((1 "John" 24000 10000) (2 "Paul" 1000 0)
   (3 "George" 5000 10000))
  ```

- An illegal transfer is then attempted: Paul has no permitted overdraft and tries to transfer more than his balance. First, the pre-condition, prototyped by a similar process, may be evaluated:

```
.> (pre-transf 2 1 10000 am)
NIL
```

REFINE being constructed upon LISP, NIL corresponds to false; the pre-condition is thus not fulfilled by these input values. An attempt to perform the transfer results in:

```
.> (transf 2 1 10000)
Error: Received signal number 11 (Segmentation violation)
```

Actually, the semantics of VDM operations mean that if an operation is started with a false pre-condition, anything may happen! In fact, TRANSF has called TRANSF-F which has returned undefined; then an error occurred as the interpreter tried to extract the first field of this value.

2.3.2.   The VDM Animator

In order to facilitate this animation, the KIDS/VDM environment provides a graphical interface to the prototype (Fig. 2). The "VDM animator" visualizes the metaphor of the abstract machine. The abstract machine stores internal variables that are affected by its operations. The *State Variables* window displays the current contents of the internal state (here, variable AM). The operations of the abstract machine appear as mouse-sensitive words in the *Buttons* window. The user may click on these buttons to apply the operations to the machine. The contents of the *State Variables* window are updated accordingly. Operations may also take additional input parameters and deliver some output values through the *Input* and *Output* windows.

The VDM animator is automatically instantiated from the text of the corresponding VDM specification. The buttons and variables are then linked to the REFINE variables and functions produced by the prototyping process.

In practice, the VDM animator provides an easy way to experiment with the resulting prototype. The user has a comprehensive look at all variables of its specification, provided that these fit into a single window, and has a user-friendly access to its operations. Nevertheless, this interface suffers serious limitations to scale up.

- When the specification includes a large number of operations, the user needs a more structured access to the *Buttons* window than the current linear menu. Also, it would be interesting to highlight applicable operations, i.e. the ones whose pre-conditions may be fulfilled by the current state provided adequate input values are given.

- When the number of variables or their size scales up, a textual description of the contents is not sufficient. For example, if the *am* variable included 1000 bank accounts, it would be difficult to extract the relevant information from the *State Variables* window. One way to cope with this problem is to ask the developer to provide an application dependent interface to these data structures. But the development cost of this special purpose interface is not always compatible with a rapid prototyping approach.

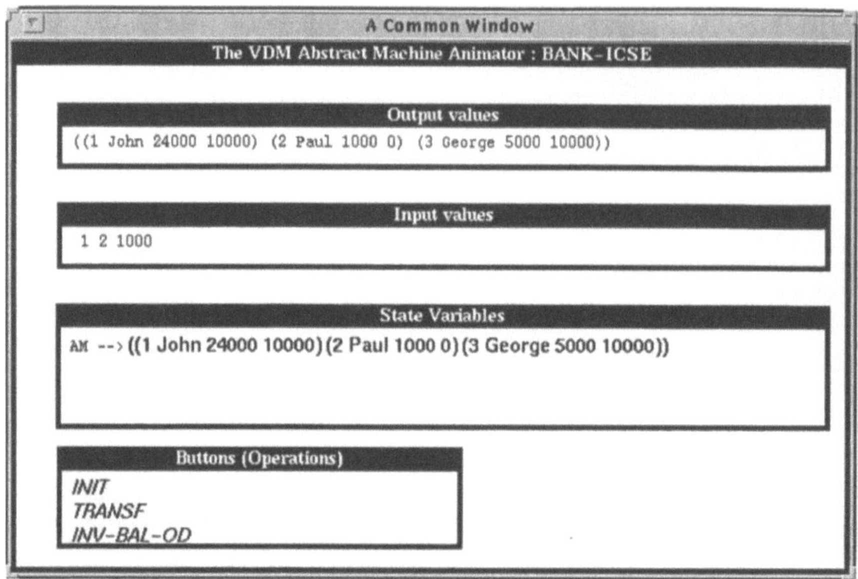

Figure 2. The VDM animator

3. Refinements of the specification

The VDM method allows one to refine abstract specifications into more concrete ones. This refinement mechanism is usually considered as a way to link specifications to programs but it may also be used to further develop specifications. In this case study of bank transfer, both refinements of control structures and data structures are presented. First the debit and credit operations are introduced, then the data structure representing an account is further developed.

3.1. *Refining the control flow*

The specification of the bank transfer proceeds with the decomposition of $TRANSF$ into $DEBIT$ and $CREDIT$. This decomposition is intended to model the following statement of the bank code:

When you pay a cheque into your bank account at the branch where you have your account, the amount of the cheque will be shown on your statement as being credited to your account on that day. So the value of the cheque appears to be available for you to use immediately.

Therefore, the transfer may be specified as a sequential combination of operations:

$$TRANSF(fr, to, a) \triangleq CREDIT(fr, to, a); DEBIT(fr, to, a)$$

In order to make the amount of the cheque directly available, the credit operation is performed first; the debit takes place when the cheque has been processed completely. This models the corresponding statement:

The cheque has to be sent to the branch of the bank on which it is drawn.

The specifications of $CREDIT$ and $DEBIT$ result from the split of the pre- and post-conditions of $TRANSF$. The pre-condition of $CREDIT$ states that the credited account number must exist and is different from the debited account. Its post-condition expresses the modification of the am map.

$CREDIT\ (fr\_ac: Acno, to\_ac: Acno, a: \mathbb{N}_1)$

ext wr $am\ :\ Acno \xrightarrow{m} Acdata$

pre $to\_ac \in \textbf{dom}\ am \land fr\_ac \neq to\_ac$

post $am = \overleftarrow{am} \dagger \{to\_ac \mapsto \mu(\overleftarrow{am}(to\_ac), bal \mapsto bal(\overleftarrow{am}(to\_ac)) + a)\}$

Similarly, the pre-condition of $DEBIT$ ensures that the debited account exists, that it is different from the credited account, and that its balance and overdraft limit allow the transfer to take place. The post-condition expresses the modification of the am map.

$DEBIT\ (fr\_ac: Acno, to\_ac: Acno, a: \mathbb{N}_1)$

ext wr $am\ :\ Acno \xrightarrow{m} Acdata$

pre $fr\_ac \in \textbf{dom}\ am \land fr\_ac \neq to\_ac \land bal(am(fr\_ac))-a \geq -od(am(fr\_ac))$

post $am = \overleftarrow{am} \dagger \{fr\_ac \mapsto \mu(\overleftarrow{am}(fr\_ac), bal \mapsto bal(\overleftarrow{am}(fr\_ac))-a)\}$

Using Hoare Logic or the logic of VDM, it is possible to show that the sequential combination of these operations is a valid implementation of $TRANSF$. But before performing this proof, the developer may want to convince himself that this refinement has the expected behaviour by animating it. So the transfer of 1000 between accounts 1 and 2 corresponds to the following sequential execution.

```
.> am
((1 "John" 25000 10000) (2 "Paul" 0 0) (3 "George" 5000 10000))
.> (credit 1 2 1000)
((1 "John" 25000 10000) (2 "Paul" 1000 0) (3 "George" 5000 10000))
.> (debit 1 2 1000)
((1 "John" 24000 10000) (2 "Paul" 1000 0) (3 "George" 5000 10000))
.>
```

This combination of operations produces the same result as the single execution of *TRANSF*. Obviously, a single test case is not sufficient to demonstrate the correctness of the refinement. Moreover, although implementation freedom tends to be limited in banking applications, a specification may admit several correct refinements with different behaviours. Nevertheless, these tests provide clues on the correctness of the decomposition. Being convinced of the correctness of his refinement, the developer may then proceed with its formal proof.

3.2. Refining the data structures

A careful examination of the trace of the previous animation reveals that, after the execution of *CREDIT*, the total amount of money recorded on the accounts of John and Paul (26000) is greater than the amount effectively stored in the bank (25000). The developer may suspect some error in his specification, as confirmed by a careful reading of the bank rules:

> *The money is not immediately transferred from the account of the writer of the cheque to your own account. Instead, the cheque has to be sent to the branch of the bank on which it is drawn. Only when the account of the writer of the cheque is debited is the value of the cheque transferred to your account - this process is called 'clearing' the cheque. While the cheque is being processed it is described as 'uncleared for interest'; when you actually receive the value of the cheque it is described as 'cleared for interest'.*

> . . .

> *What is important for you is that if you withdraw the money from your account before the cheque is 'cleared for interest', you may become overdrawn for the purpose of calculating interest and you will then be charged interest on this overdraft.*

Instead of performing a further refinement of the control flow, the developer decides to refine his data structures in order to introduce an "effective balance" field (*ebal*) in *Acdata*. This effective balance corresponds to the amount cleared for interest.

$Acno = \mathbb{N}$

$$
\begin{aligned}
Acdata \; :: \; & own \; : \; char^* \\
& bal \; : \; \mathbb{Z} \\
& ebal \; : \; \mathbb{Z} \\
& od \; : \; \mathbb{N}
\end{aligned}
$$

inv $(mk\text{-}Acdata(own, bal, ebal, od)) \triangleq bal \geq \text{-}od \land bal \geq ebal$

The invariant associated with this new data type still enforces the relation between balance and overdraft. It also states that the effective balance is always lower than or equal to the balance. This means that the customer never has more on his account than reported, but may have less money than he thinks and subsequently might pay unexpected interest charges.

In order to prove that this refinement is correct, the developer must provide a "retrieve function" which returns the abstract representation from the concrete one. In this case, the retrieve function is obvious: it only masks the *ebal* field of the concrete representation. The developer must then prove several mathematical properties of this function (e.g. for every valid abstract value, a concrete representation may be found). Here, the animation facilities of the KIDS/VDM environment don't really help.

Still, the refinement of the data structures also impacts on the specification of the associated operations. *CREDIT* and *DEBIT* should be refined in order to conveniently update the *ebal* field of the accounts. Two alternate refinements may be considered at this stage.

In the first refinement, the *CREDIT*1 operation simply affects the balance. The effective balance remains unchanged; its modification only takes place when *DEBIT*1 is performed.

$CREDIT1\ (fr\_ac: Acno, to\_ac: Acno, a: \mathbb{N}_1)$

ext wr $am\ :\ Acno \xrightarrow{m} Acdata$

pre $to\_ac \in \textbf{dom}\ am \wedge fr\_ac \neq to\_ac$

post $am = \overleftarrow{am} \dagger \{to\_ac \mapsto \mu(\overleftarrow{am}(to\_ac), bal \mapsto bal(\overleftarrow{am}(to\_ac)) + a)\}$

$DEBIT1\ (fr\_ac: Acno, to\_ac: Acno, a: \mathbb{N}_1)$

ext wr $am\ :\ Acno \xrightarrow{m} Acdata$

pre $fr\_ac \in \textbf{dom}\ am \wedge fr\_ac \neq to\_ac$
$\wedge bal(am(fr\_ac))\text{-}a \geq \text{-}od(am(fr\_ac))$

post $am = \overleftarrow{am} \dagger \{fr\_ac \mapsto \mu(\mu(\overleftarrow{am}(fr\_ac), bal \mapsto bal(\overleftarrow{am}(fr\_ac))\text{-}a),$
$$ebal \mapsto ebal(\overleftarrow{am}(fr\_ac))\text{-}a),$$
$$to\_ac \mapsto \mu(\overleftarrow{am}(to\_ac), ebal \mapsto ebal(\overleftarrow{am}(to\_ac)) + a)\}$$

The animation gives thus the following trace[2]: *CREDIT*1 only modifies Paul's account and *DEBIT*1 modifies both. As far as the *own*, *bal*, and *od* field are concerned, the results of both abstract and concrete operations are identical.

```
.> (init)
((1 "John" 25000 25000 10000) (2 "Paul" 0 0 0))
.> (credit1 1 2 1000)
((1 "John" 25000 25000 10000) (2 "Paul" 1000 0 0))
.> (debit1 1 2 1000)
((1 "John" 24000 24000 10000) (2 "Paul" 1000 1000 0))
```

In the second possible refinement, the transferred amount is immediately debited from the effective balance of *fr_ac* when *CREDIT*2 takes place. It is only credited to *to_ac* at the execution of *DEBIT*2. As far as the effective balance is concerned *CREDIT*2 is a debit operation and *DEBIT*2 is a credit: the transfer is in fact a sequence of debit followed by credit.

$CREDIT2\ (fr\_ac: Acno, to\_ac: Acno, a: \mathbb{N}_1)$

ext wr $am\ :\ Acno \xrightarrow{m} Acdata$

pre $to\_ac \in \textbf{dom}\ am \wedge fr\_ac \neq to\_ac$

post $am = \overleftarrow{am} \dagger \{fr\_ac \mapsto \mu(\overleftarrow{am}(fr\_ac), ebal \mapsto ebal(\overleftarrow{am}(fr\_ac))\text{-}a),$
$$to\_ac \mapsto \mu(\overleftarrow{am}(to\_ac), bal \mapsto bal(\overleftarrow{am}(to\_ac)) + a)\}$$

$DEBIT2\ (fr\_ac\colon Acno, to\_ac\colon Acno, a\colon \mathbb{N}_1)$

ext wr $am\ \colon\ Acno \xrightarrow{m} Acdata$

pre $fr\_ac \in \mathbf{dom}\ am \wedge fr\_ac \neq to\_ac$
$\qquad \wedge\ bal(am(fr\_ac))\text{-}a \geq \text{-}od(am(fr\_ac))$

post $am = \overleftarrow{am}\ \dagger\ \{fr\_ac \mapsto \mu(\overleftarrow{am}(fr\_ac), bal \mapsto bal(\overleftarrow{am}(fr\_ac))\text{-}a),$
$\qquad\qquad\qquad to\_ac \mapsto \mu(\overleftarrow{am}(to\_ac), ebal \mapsto ebal(\overleftarrow{am}(to\_ac)) + a)\}$

The animation confirms this understanding of the specification: after $CREDIT2$ the total amount of money recorded on the effective balances is lower than the amount of money stored in the bank. Once again, one may compare abstract and concrete behaviours to get clues on the correctness of the refinement.

```
.> (init)
((1 "John" 25000 25000 10000) (2 "Paul" 0 0 0))
.> (credit2 1 2 1000)
((1 "John" 25000 24000 10000) (2 "Paul" 1000 0 0))
.> (debit2 1 2 1000)
((1 "John" 24000 24000 10000) (2 "Paul" 1000 1000 0))
```

Deciding which of these alternate concrete refinements is the right one is out of the scope of this paper. Presumably, this decision, which is mainly a business concern, will result from a discussion between the developer and a representative of the bank. The animation of the specification may help the communication between these persons.

During this dialog, new problems may arise like the following one. This trace shows how the interleaving of two transactions may lead Paul to a negative effective balance.

```
.> (init)
((1 "John" 25000 25000 10000) (2 "Paul" 0 0 0)
 (3 "George" 5000 5000 10000))
.> (credit2 1 2 15000)
((1 "John" 25000 10000 10000) (2 "Paul" 15000 0 0)
 (3 "George" 5000 5000 10000))
.> (credit2 2 3 10000)
((1 "John" 25000 10000 10000) (2 "Paul" 5000 -10000 0)
 (3 "George" 15000 5000 10000))
.> (debit2 2 3 10000)
((1 "John" 25000 10000 10000) (2 "Paul" 5000 -10000 0)
 (3 "George" 15000 15000 10000))
.> (debit2 1 2 15000)
((1 "John" 10000 10000 10000) (2 "Paul" 5000 5000 0)
 (3 "George" 15000 15000 10000))
```

It reveals a problem in the code of the bank: Paul will have to pay interest charges but, since he has no permitted overdraft, he never signed any agreement with the bank on the charged interest rates!

4. Conclusions

4.1. Uses of prototyping

The presentation of this case study has tried to demonstrate how a specification process may benefit from a prototyping tool. The use of this tool may take several forms:

Dialog support. It supports the dialog between a specifier and his customer. The execution of a prototype is usually closer to the customer's concerns than the mathematical statement of the specification. In the bank transfer case study, this interaction with the customer is needed to choose between $CREDIT1$ and $CREDIT2$.

Understanding. It helps the developer understand his specification because it leads him to take a different viewpoint at his specification than the purely mathematical viewpoint. For example, the animation of $CREDIT$ leads to discover that there is more money on the accounts than in the bank.

Error detection. The syntactical checks, the development, or the execution of the prototype may fail and reveal an error in the specification. In this case study, an error was detected in the original specification of C. Jones: the precondition of $TRANSF$ stated that $bal - a \geq od$ instead of $bal - a \geq -od$. Such a specification is too restrictive because it asks the customer to have a very positive balance before performing the transfer. This kind of error can not be detected in the formal verification of the specification; since the pre-condition is too strong, it fulfills the proof obligations. It seems that this error results from a rework of the specification where the original type of od, i.e. integer, was changed to natural.

Refinement support. Execution traces of the prototypes corresponding to abstract and concrete specifications have been compared in section 3. This provides clues on the correctness of the refinements. Provided that the prototyping activity is fast and cheap, it becomes part of a Refine-Prototype-Proof process. In this process, proof activities are only undertaken when the developer is confident in the correctness of his refinement.

Data refinement has received less attention here than operation refinement. One way to support the refinement of data structures is to synthesize executable code for the retrieve function (here, a mask on the *ebal* field). At animation time, this function is used to extract the abstract information from its concrete representation.

Tests. A record of the execution traces of the prototype may provide raw material for the definition of test scenarios for the final product.

The rigorous exploitation of these facilities necessitates methodological guidelines and support that go beyond the scope of this work.

4.2. Related work

Several attempts to prototype VDM specifications are reported in the computing literature [10] [9] [13]. ENCOMPASS [23] goes beyond prototyping to support operation decomposition, using tests and formal verification. Most of these attempts propose a translation process from a restricted form of VDM to languages close to LISP or Prolog. The restrictions on the language may affect the data structures supported or the logic of pre- and post-conditions. Actually, this logic is close to first order predicate logic, which is undecidable. Restricting it to Horn clauses is one way to make the language executable.

The ambition of KIDS/VDM is to support the full VDM specification language. In particular, the pre- and post-conditions do not suffer any restriction and can not, in full generality, be translated automatically into executable constructs. In KIDS/VDM, this undecidability problem is solved by the semi-automatic character of the program development mode. First, the user may guide the search for an algorithm by the selection of an appropriate tactic. Then, if KIDS does not include enough design knowledge about the problem to solve, the user may try to add transformation rules to the system.

The IFAD toolbox [7] is currently the most mature tool to execute VDM specifications. It is based on an executable subset of VDM, where implicit specifications in terms of pre- and post-conditions must be associated with explicit executable code. Its scope is thus different from the one of KIDS/VDM, which is based on the implicit style. Experiments with this toolbox [19] have shown that it definitely helps detect errors in specifications.

The bank transfer case study does not use this explicit style, and therefore can not be executed with this toolbox. It started from an off-the shelf specification that was not meant to be prototyped. A translation of this specification into an explicit one would not be difficult. But, as discussed in section 4.3, there is a definite risk to focus on executability concerns at specification time. Nevertheless, it is fair to mention that, in this case study, the translation of implicit specifications into code is rather straightforward. It would be easy to extend the IFAD toolbox in order to support restricted forms of implicit specification.

4.3. Limits

About 100 small VDM specifications, mostly taken from [11], have been prototyped with the tool. 80 to 90% of these have led to executable code. In order to increase this percentage, more design knowledge must be added to KIDS (definition of new tactics or new transformation rules). Also, the KIDS user interface, the interactive character of the prototyping process, and the poor support of VDM for modular specifications restrict the possibility to scale-up [16].

Since these specifications were quite simple, none has revealed a problem of code efficiency. Nevertheless, some of the prototypes are based on a global search algorithm. So, execution time and algorithmic complexity may become significant problems. These problems also exist with the other prototyping approaches listed in section 4.2. In these approaches, efficiency problems often lead to incorporate premature design decisions in specifications. In the KIDS/VDM approach, efficiency concerns are handled during the program synthesis phase where optimization tactics and simplifications performed by the theorem prover help decrease algorithmic complexity. For example, in section 2, an optimization tactic has introduced variables C-1, C-2, C-3 to avoid computing these values several times.

In section 2.3.2, the VDM animator has been presented and some of its limits were mentioned. It is an attempt to ease the animation of the prototype by a user-friendly interface. The effective use of this tool would require further extensions like:

- the systematic recording of the execution sequences with a facility to replay the sequence of operations or to browse through the state history; this would be the first step of an evolution towards a test environment;

- the possibility to execute in parallel a specification and its refinement in order to compare their behaviours.

4.4. *Contribution of Knowledge-Based tools*

The prototyping facility is based on two tools which contribute to its success:

- REFINE brings in a programming language that supports the VDM data structures and most operations on these structures. Experience with the KIDS/VDM system on about 100 specifications showed that it was close enough to VDM to provide a good target language. The bank transfer case study showed that the overriding operator was missing. But this was not a major problem since it could be easily programmed.

- KIDS brings in an environment where every step is controlled. This guarantees the correspondence between the specification and its prototype. It also allows one to record a development and to replay it afterwards.

  KIDS encapsulates design knowledge to synthesize code from specification and to further optimize code. Our experiments showed that good results could be reached in the prototyping process with a very basic design tactic (spec-to-code). This is due to the short semantical distance between VDM and REFINE and to the fact that many VDM specifications are closer to code than intended.

  Finally, KIDS provides theorem proving facilities that can be used to prove properties of VDM specifications. Experiments have shown the feasibility of these proof activities, but it is necessary to further tailor the theorem prover to the kind of proofs involved in VDM specifications.

In summary, both KIDS and REFINE provide powerful and reusable tools to KIDS/VDM.

Acknowledgments

D. Bert, P.G. Larsen, and the anonymous reviewers of JASE and KBSE have improved the quality of this paper by their comments. A. Finkelstein and M. Feather have provided the initial statement of the problem. Doug Smith and Kestrel Institute have significantly contributed to this research by introducing me to KIDS and replying to my numerous questions in the recent years. The KIDS/VDM research started at the Université Catholique de Louvain, within the Leibniz project, and continued at the Faculté Polytechnique de Mons; it is currently led at the Université Joseph Fourier within the BQR Forsud project.

Notes

1. REFINE is a trademark of REASONING SYSTEMS Inc.
2. For clarity sake, Georges's account, which remains unchanged, is not displayed in this trace.

References

1. Andrews, D., Bruun, H., Hansen, B., Larsen, P., Plat, N. et al. 1995, *Information Technology — Programming Languages, their environments and system software interfaces — Vienna Development Method-Specification Language Part 1: Base language*, ISO.
2. Barclays Bank PLC, . 1991, The Barclays code of business banking, Barclays Bank, Commercial Banking Division.
3. Bicarregui, J. C., Fitzgerald, J. S., Lindsay, P. A., Moore, R. and Ritchie, B. 1994, *Proof in VDM: A Practitioner's Guide*, FACIT, Springer-Verlag.
4. Bowen, J. and Stavridou, V. 1992, Safety-critical systems, formal methods and standards, *Technical Report PRG-TR-5-92*, Oxford University Computing Laboratory.
5. Chung, L., Nixon, B. and Yu, E. 1995, Using non-functional requirements to systematically support change, *RE '95 - Second IEEE international symposium on Requirements Engineering*.
6. Craigen, D., Gerhart, S. and Ralston, T. 1993, An international survey of industrial applications of formal methods, *Technical Report NISTGCR 93/626*, U.S. National Institute of Standards and technology.
7. Elmstrom, R., Larsen, P. G. and Lassen, P. B. 1994, The IFAD VDM-SL toolbox : a practical approach to formal specifications, *ACM SIGPLAN Notices* **29**(9), 77–80.
8. Hayes, I. J. and Jones, C. B. 1989, Specifications are not (necessarily) executable, *IEE, Software Engineering Journal* **4**(6), 320–338.
9. Hekmatpour, S. and Ince, D. 1988, *Software prototyping, formal methods and VDM*, Addison-Wesley.
10. Henderson, P. 1986, Functional programming, formal specification, and rapid prototyping, *IEEE Transactions on Software Engineering* **12**(2), 241–250.
11. Jones, C. B. 1990, *Systematic Software Development Using VDM (Second Edition)*, Prentice-Hall, London.
12. Jones, C., Jones, K., Lindsay, P. and Moore, R. 1991, *Mural: A Formal Development Support System*, Springer-Verlag.
13. Kans, A. and Hayton, C. 1994, Using ABC to prototype VDM specifications, *ACM SIGPLAN Notices* **29**(1), 27–37.
14. Larsen, P. G. 1994, Response to "the formal specification of safety requirements for storing explosives", *Formal Aspects of Computing* **6**(5), 565–568.
15. Ledru, Y. 1994, Proof-based development of specifications with KIDS/VDM, *in* M. Naftalin, T. Denvir and M. Bertran (eds), *FME'94: Industrial Benefit of Formal Methods*, Vol. 873 of *Lecture Notes in Computer Science*, Springer-Verlag, pp. 214–232.
16. Ledru, Y. 1996, Using KIDS as a tool support for VDM, *Proceedings of the 18th International Conference on Software Engineering*, IEEE Computer Society Press.
17. Ledru, Y. and Liégeois, M.-H. 1991, Integrating REFINE prototypes in a VDM development framework, *in* B. Möller (ed.), *Proceedings of the IFIP TC2 Working conference on Constructing Programs from Specifications*, North-Holland, pp. 243–265.
18. Ledru, Y. and Liégeois, M.-H. 1992, Prototyping VDM specifications with KIDS, *Proceedings of the 7th Knowledge-Based Software Engineering Conference*, IEEE Computer Society Press, pp. 50–59.
19. Mukherjee, P. 1995, Computer-aided validation of formal specifications, *IEE, Software Engineering Journal* pp. 133–140.

20. Smith, D. 1990, KIDS: a semi-automatic program development system, *IEEE Transactions on Software Engineering — Special Issue on Formal Methods* **16**(9), 1024–1043.
21. Smith, D., Kotik, G. and Westfold, S. 1985, Research on Knowledge-Based Software Environments at Kestrel Institute, *IEEE Transactions on Software Engineering* **11**(11), 1278–1295.
22. Spivey, J. 1992, *The Z notation - A Reference Manual (Second Edition)*, Prentice Hall.
23. Terwilliger, R. B. and Campbell, R. H. 1989, ENCOMPASS: An environment for the incremental development of software, *The Journal of Systems and Software* **10**, 41–53.

Automated Software Engineering 4, 53–75 (1997)

Interactive Explanation of Software Systems

W. LEWIS JOHNSON   johnson@isi.edu
ALI ERDEM   erdem@isi.edu
USC/Information Sciences Institute & Computer Science Dept., 4676 Admiralty Way, Marina del Rey, CA 90292-6695

Abstract.   This paper describes an effort to provide automated support for the interactive inquiry and explanation process that is at the heart of software understanding. A hypermedia tool called I-Doc allows software engineers to post queries about a software system, and generates focused explanations in response. These explanations are *task oriented*, i.e., they are sensitive to the software engineering task being performed by the user that led to the query. Task orientation leads to more effective explanations, and is particularly helpful for understanding large software systems. Empirical studies of inquiry episodes were conducted in order to investigate this claim: the kinds of questions users ask, their relation to the user's task and level of expertise. The I-Doc tool is being developed to embody these principles, employing knowledge-based techniques. The presentation mechanism employs World Wide Web (WWW) technology, making it suitable for widespread use.

Keywords: software explanation, software understanding, hypertext, World Wide Web

1.   Introduction and motivation

Software engineers, and software maintainers in particular, spend significant amounts of time attempting to understand software artifacts (Corbi, 1990). These software understanding activities have been characterized by Brooks (1983) and Soloway et al. (1988) as being composed of inquiry episodes. According to Soloway et al. (1988), inquiry episodes involve the following steps: *read* some code, ask a *question* about the code, *conjecture* an answer, and *search* the documentation and code for confirmation of the conjecture. Because of the important roles that conjecture and search play in the process, Selfridge has described software understanding as a discovery process (Selfridge, 1990).

Search in software understanding is very error-prone; people do not always know where to look for information to support their conjectures. In Soloway's studies the most successful subjects systematically scanned code and documentation from beginning to end, to make sure they found the information they required. This is clearly impractical for large systems.

The solution that Soloway and others advocate is to organize documentation to make search easier. Two principal methods have been attempted. One is to *link* documentation, so that the understander can easily get from the site in the documents where the question is posed to the site where the answer can be found. Soloway uses this technique to document delocalized plans, linking the various elements of the plan together. The other method is to *layer* documentation, so that different types of information reside in different layers. For example, Rajlich (Rajlich et al., 1994) organizes information into a problem domain layer, an algorithm layer, and a representation layer. Understanders can then limit their reading and searching to particular layers. The conjecture-and-search method of obtaining answers to questions is essentially unchanged in these approaches, but the search process is made more efficient.

Of course there is another common technique for obtaining answers to inquiries about software—to ask somebody who knows. There is no need for searching at all with this method. Our objective is to develop a tool that approaches the ideal of having an expert on hand to answer questions. Such a tool should be able to respond directly to the user's inquiry with information that helps provide an answer.

Research in automating consultative dialogs has identified a number of important requirements for explanation systems (Moore, 1995). First, they must, of course, have the necessary knowledge to provide the desired answers. Second, they must provide answers in a form that the questioner can understand and avoid concepts that the questioner is unfamiliar with. Third, they should take into account the goals of the questioner. The content of the answer can depend upon what the user is trying to do with the information.

Principles similar to these are already the basis for the design of certain types of user manuals, namely minimal manuals (Lazonder and Meij, 1993). Such manuals attempt to anticipate the tasks that users might need to perform, and provide information to help achieve them. Although advocates of minimal manuals claim that novice users are in particular need of task oriented documentation, it is reasonable to hypothesize that software professionals would benefit as well. Lakhotia (1993), for example, quotes a software developer who says that what he would like in the way of a software understanding tool is "something that helps me get the job done, fast". Unfortunately, the tasks of software professionals in general are not precisely defined. User manuals can be oriented toward specific tasks, such as composing a letter or generating a mailing list. Software engineering tasks such as design or maintenance are much broader, and the influence of such tasks on software understanding is unclear, although software understanding researchers such as Brooks have conjectured that such influences exist (Brooks, 1983).

In order to develop tools that approach the ideal of an on-line software consultant, our work has proceeded on two thrusts. First, we have examined the interactions that occur during expert consultations, in order to determine what types of questions people ask and what governs the answers the experts provide. We have been particularly interested in the following.

- What kinds of information do people ask for?
- How does user task and expertise influence the question?
- What information about the questioner (e.g., task, level of expertise), determines the form of the answer?
- To what extent is the information available from conventional documentation sources?

Second, we are using these results to revise and enhance the implementation of an on-line documentation tool called Intelligent Documentation (I-Doc). An initial version of I-Doc was built prior to the empirical study with task orientation in mind. The results of the empirical study helped us in clarifying the relation between user tasks and questions, and in building a taxonomy of question types.

Information provided by I-Doc is explicitly organized in the form of answers to common questions. Like most expert consulting systems, and unlike typical on-line documentation, the system has an explicit model of the user and his or her task. This enables the system to select information that is likely to be useful, and present it in an appropriate form. The objective is to increase the likelihood that the information provided answers the user's question, and to reduce the amount of search and interpretation required. The presentation medium being employed is *dynamic hypertext*, i.e., hypertext descriptions that are created dynamically in response to user queries. Automated text generation techniques can make hypertext a medium for human-computer dialog, with features similar to that of interactive question answering systems. The hypertext descriptions are presented using commonly available tools, namely World Wide Web (WWW) clients.

2. Empirical study

2.1. Motivation

In order to obtain a realistic picture of the software inquiry process, it is desirable to focus on the task of understanding large, complex systems. Most investigations of software understanding, such as Soloway's study of JPL (Soloway et al., 1988) or Rajlich's study (Rajlich et al., 1994), concern themselves instead with small programs, of 500 lines or less. However, the task of understanding a small program is likely to be different from that of understanding a large program. For example, Soloway found in his study that the people who did best in understanding software read the code linearly from beginning to end; this approach becomes impractical as codes become larger. Unfortunately, as the size of programs increases, so does the amount of time required to understand the software. This makes it difficult to collect data from large numbers of subjects.

We therefore decided to examine a different source of data on software inquiries, namely the messages posted to Usenet newsgroups on software-related topics. We were particularly interested in the hierarchy of newsgroups under comp.lang, which contain discussions about programming languages. The articles posted to comp.lang newsgroups include a wide range of questions about programming problems and answers to them. The dialog between the questioner and the advisor is clearly observable from these messages. The variety in questioners' backgrounds, expertise and activities make these newsgroups good candidates for studying the software inquiries.

We focused our attention on the comp.lang.tcl newsgroup, which contains discussions about Tcl and Tk programming languages. Tcl is a simple textual language and a library package. Its ease of use and simplicity makes it useful for writing shell scripts and prototyping applications. Tk is an extension of Tcl and provides the programmer with an interface to the X11 windowing system. When these tools are used together, it is possible to develop GUI applications quickly. The source code and the documentation for both systems are available to the users. However, because of both the limitations of the documentation and the frequent upgrades to these products, some users still rely on the newsgroup to get answers to their questions.

Tcl and Tk are fairly large in terms of their source code size. Tcl version 7.4 has 25,902 lines of C code, 2,707 lines in the header files and 8659 lines of documentation. Tk version 4.0 has 86,782 lines of C code, 7,382 lines in the header files and 25,219 lines of documentation.

Another advantage of studying Tcl/Tk newsgroup was the availability of the source code and the documentation to the users. It was possible for the users to answer some of the questions by looking at the source code, which is reasonably well documented and easy to understand. In particular, the code developers made an effort to explain the purpose of each procedure and data element, summarize key algorithms, explain the intent behind specific statements within the code, and note where assumptions are being made about processing elsewhere in the system. This resulted in some interesting messages in which users refer to the source code or the documentation. It also gave us some data for investigating where the users search an answer, in the source code or in the documentation, and under what conditions.

2.2. Data analysis

1250 messages posted to the newsgroup between 2/17/95 and 4/22/95 were analyzed. The data analysis method was similar to that used by Herbsleb and Kuwana (1993). Only messages that asked questions about Tcl/Tk were considered. Messages asking irrelevant questions (distribution sites, FAQ location etc.), product announcements, and opinions were ignored. The message set included 249 questions, which were categorized along multiple dimensions. Answers were noted, but were not explicitly categorized as part of this particular investigation.

For each question, the questioner's level of expertise was estimated. In nearly all cases, the expertise level was easily inferred. It was either stated explicitly in the message or was easily guessed by looking at the contents of the message. If the questioner stated that he just started learning Tcl/Tk or asked a very simple question that was covered in the documentation, we classified him as a novice. If he had been using Tcl/Tk for more than a year or asked complex questions that were not in the documentation, he was classified as an expert. All others were classified as intermediates. Of the 249 questions, 55 was asked by novices, 185 by intermediates and 9 by experts.

Next, the questioner's task was categorized. It was useful to characterize tasks at two levels: the *macrotask* and *microtask* levels. A macrotask is an activity that someone performs on the system as a whole, e.g., maintaining it. A microtask is a more local activity performed on a specific system component or artifact, e.g., forking a process, configuring a widget, or invoking the **make** utility.

Inferring the microtasks from the messages was easier than inferring the macrotasks. The questioners usually indicated what they were trying to do. This particular study did not attempt to categorize the types of microtasks, but did record the subject of the questions, i.e., the component that was the focus of the microtask.

In attempting to classify the macrotasks, it was evident that it would not be possible to come up with a mutually exclusive set of macrotask definitions that would not be open to dispute. For example, what we might consider to be maintenance activity could be considered as programming activity by others. To minimize this problem, we classified the users into three easily distinguishable categories, *installers*, *users* and *programmers*. We further divided the programmers into 4 different groups depending on the domain of the problem they were trying to solve. For example, if the user asked a question about a Tk widget, then we classified him as a GUI programmer.

This resulted in the following macrotask categorization:

- *Installer*: Users who are installing or upgrading Tcl/Tk
- *User*: Users of Tcl/Tk applications who focus not on the programming issues, but usage problems, e.g., *Why can't I use enter in buttons?*
- *Integration programmer*: Programmers who are trying to integrate Tcl/Tk with C by calling Tcl/Tk functions from C or vice versa
- *GUI programmer*: Programmers who focus on graphical user interface issues
- *Communication programmer*: Programmers who develop applications that communicate with other applications running on the same or a remote computer
- *Other programmers*: All other programmers including UNIX shell programmers

After the questioner's expertise level and task were determined, the type of question was classified. Other researchers have tried to classify user questions before. For example, Wright claimed that user's questions are either task oriented or symptom oriented (Wright, 1988). Hill and Miller studied the types of questions asked by users of an experimental graphical statistics program (Hill and Miller, 1988) and they categorized the questions as requests for plans to achieve task-specific goals; describe or identify system object; verify action as proper; describe system capability etc. However, these researchers focused mainly on questions from software users, whereas the questions in the Tcl/Tk data set come primarily from programmers. As a result, the categorization scheme used here differs slightly from those used in the above studies.

Questions were classified as *goal oriented*, *symptom oriented*, and *system oriented*.

- *Goal oriented*: These questions requested help to achieve task-specific goals and were further categorized as follows:

  - *Plan request*: Questions like *How can I read a file into an array?* asked for a plan to achieve the goal.
  - *Goal satisfiability*: An example question in this group was *Is it possible to display a picture on a button widget?* These questions differed from the plan requests, since the user was not sure whether the goal was achievable. However, usually the answers to both types of questions included the plans to achieve the goal.

- *Symptom oriented*: When the users could not identify the source of a problem, they asked these questions. An example was *Tcl installation fails with an error message. What am I doing wrong?*
- *System oriented*: These questions requested information for identification of system objects and functions. They consisted of:

  - *Motivational*: The users tried to understand why the system functioned in a particular way and how that behavior could be useful. An example was *Why is the ability to bind to the CreateNotify and DestroyNotify events not supported in Tk bind command?*

— *Conceptual*: These questions asked for descriptions of system objects and functions. An example was *What is an option menu?*
— *Explanatory*: These questions requested explanations about how the system worked, e.g., *How does auto_path variable work?*

In addition to these categorizations, we also noted whether the message contained any examples and if they were general or specific descriptions. Code samples and error messages were classified as specific, the descriptions of the desired outcome with no specific information were classified as general.

Finally we identified the target for each question in order to find out the relations between the question type, the level of expertise and the target. As in Herbsleb and Kuwana's study (1993), we defined target as the subject of the question.

2.3. Results and discussion

After all the messages were classified, the number of messages in each group were counted. Table 1 summarizes the distribution of questions by macrotask, expertise and question types.

2.3.1. What kinds of information do people ask for?

There were 3 major groups of questions in our classification: *goal oriented, symptom oriented* and *system oriented*. Among these, goal oriented questions occurred most frequently. The users usually knew what they wanted to achieve, but did not know how to accomplish it.

Symptom oriented questions were asked less often than the goal oriented ones, but they still constituted almost one-fourth of all questions. The users lacked the necessary knowledge to diagnose the problem in their code or the system's operation, and asked for this missing information. The answerers usually knew the solution, because they experienced a similar problem before and found the solution.

Table 1. The distribution of messages by task, expertise and question type (N: Novice, I: Intermediate, E: Expert).

Macrotasks	Goal oriented						Symptom			System oriented									Task total
	Plan request			Goal			Symptom			Motivat.			Concept.			Explan.			
	N	I	E	N	I	E	N	I	E	N	I	E	N	I	E	N	I	E	total
Installer							7	2											9
User				2	2					2			1						7
Integrator	5	4			2		1	6										1	19
GUI prog.	11	65	5	5	34	1	4	25			5		1	1		1	3		161
Comm. prog.		3	1					2									1		7
Other prog.	5	14		2	5	1	5	7						1		3	3		46
Total	21	86	6	9	43	2	17	42		2	5		2	2		4	7	1	249
Type total (%)	113 (45%)			54 (22%)			59 (24%)			7 (2%)			4 (2%)			12 (5%)			
Section total	167 (67%)						59 (24%)			23 (9%)									

Finally, there were questions concerned with identifying what the system objects were, how they worked and why they were necessary. The number of the system oriented questions in Tcl/Tk newsgroup was small compared to the goal and the symptom oriented questions. This was probably because of bias in the data. Newsgroup members may have been reluctant to ask questions that should be answerable by examining available code and documentation. Actually, the fact that system oriented questions occurred at all is an indication that available documentation suffered from limitations. If this is true for carefully documented code such as Tcl/Tk, it must be even more true for software in general.

The results of our study agree to some extent with the other researcher's results. In Hill and Miller's study (1988) goal oriented questions were 70%, system oriented questions were 22% and problem oriented questions were 4% of the total questions. In our study, problem oriented questions were more common (24%) probably due to the nature of the programming activity, but goal oriented (67%) questions were asked as much. System oriented questions had a higher percentage in their study, because the only available documentation was the advisor's help.

An important observation was the amount of experience sharing in answering questions. Usually, the answerer knew the solution as a result of his prior experience. For example, someone from Germany asked how to display umlauts in entry widgets and not surprisingly the answer also came from there. It seems possible to answer a significant portion of the questions by storing and retrieving other users' experiences.

2.3.2. *How does user task and expertise influence the question?*

The type of question users ask is predictable to a certain extent if users' task and expertise level is known. For example, installers were more likely to ask symptom oriented questions than others. This might be due to the fact that most installers were new users and didn't know enough to identify the problems. Besides, some of the installation problems were complex and required extensive knowledge outside user domain, such as details of the UNIX operating system, libraries etc. Another factor that possibly contributed to this behavior was the lack of explanations in the installation instructions. Since the installers were simply following the instructions they didn't have a good mental model of the installation process and when it failed, it was hard to identify the source of the problem.

Task by itself was not the only determiner of the question type. Expertise level was also important. Figure 1 shows the percentage distributions of question types by expertise level.

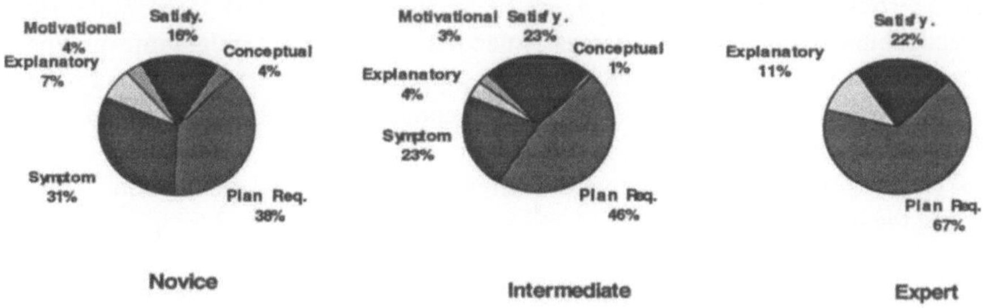

Figure 1.   Distribution of question types for different expertise levels.

It can be seen that more conceptual and motivational questions were asked by novices. As users became more familiar with the system, they asked fewer questions and the questions they did ask were more likely to be goal oriented. Symptom oriented questions became less frequent, as programmers developed an experience base of common symptoms and their causes. System oriented questions decreased from 15% for novices to 8% for intermediates. Questioner's knowledge about system objects at this level was high enough to reduce the number of conceptual and motivational questions, but was not high enough to eliminate explanatory questions. For experts, system oriented questions increased to 11% mainly because of the explanatory questions.

Although experts ask fewer questions, these ones that they do ask are more complex and harder to answer. For example, a novice plan request like *How can I display bitmaps on a button?* is easier to answer than an expert plan request like *How can I scroll the text in a widget during test selection?* We haven't attempted to measure the complexity of the targets, but target attributes like complexity and generality affect both presentation (e.g., present simple concepts before complex ones) and content (e.g., do not present complex concepts to novice users) of the documentation.

2.3.3. *What information about the questioner determines the form of the answer?* This particular study did not classify and analyze the form of the answers in detail. However, from perusing the answers that were sent in response to the posed questions, it was evident that task and expertise level were inferable from the message and this information affected the form of the answer. Frequently novice users only got the pointers to the documentation whereas experts usually received more detailed and explanatory answers.

The way the questions were asked, possibly because of individual differences, also affected the form of the answer. Some users requested brief information whereas some others wanted detailed answers with explanations. For example in the following message, the user was not only interested in identifying the problem but also wanted to learn how open worked.

> *I am trying to talk to a process by opening a pipe as described in the*
> *Tcl book (set f [open —prog r+])*
> *prog, however, wants its input in stdin only—so it exits complaining...*
> *What does really happen in "open"? Is there any way out of this?*

Soloway et al. found that users employed two macrostrategies for finding the answer to their questions, systematic and as-needed (Soloway et al., 1988). Systematic strategy users read all the documentation whereas as-needed strategy users sought information only when necessary. Research in behavioral theory supports this observation. It is known that when faced with a problem some people use just enough information to arrive at a feasible solution (satisficers) whereas some others gather as much information as they can (maximizers) (Hunsaker et al., 1994). Individual differences has to be taken into consideration in answering the users' questions.

2.3.4. *To what extent is the information available from conventional documentation sources?* Half of the questions could have been answered by consulting the documentation or source code. However, Td/Tk experience and expertise was necessary to answer the

other half. A simple looking question like *Is it possible to do multitasking in Tcl?* required extensive Tcl and programming knowledge.

Searching the source code was easier when the program code that implemented the answer was localized. The answer to the question *How can I put an image on a button?* was easier to find than *Is it possible to deactivate the toplevel window until another event?*, because Tk code was structured around graphical objects. The documentation, which was structured similarly, was probably easy to maintain, but it didn't make finding the answer to the second question easier. Documentation that supported delocalized plans could have shortened the time to find the answer (Soloway et al., 1988).

The information that needs to be delocalized depends on the task and in practice separate documentation is required for different tasks, e.g., programmer's manual, maintenance manual etc. There is considerable information overlap between these manuals, and duplicating the same information in different documents introduces the maintainability problem. A change in the system behavior requires updates to many documents. Storing the information in an online question answering system's repository and generating the documents on demand solves both the maintainability and the delocalization problems.

It was impossible to find the answers to certain questions in the documentation, since they were either asking for high level plans or instances of a general plan. A question like *How can I split canvas into pages and print?* asked for a high level plan. The answer to the question *How can I pass an array from Tcl to C?* could be answered easily if one knows that Tcl is a string based language and it is possible to pass these strings to C and do data conversion. Once a person learns this general plan, it is simple to answer questions like *How can I pass < data – type > from Tcl to C?* Although it might not be feasible to include the answer to each data-type specific question in static documentation, it is easy to generate the answers to these questions in a dynamic documentation environment.

2.3.5. Importance of examples.   Examples had an important role in both questioners' and answerers' messages. Table 2 summarizes the number of examples seen in the messages by question type.

Table 2.   Distribution of examples by question type.

Question type	No example	General description	Specific description
Plan request	54 (48%)	22 (19%)	37 (33%)
Goal satisfiable	27 (50%)	16 (30%)	11 (20%)
Symptom oriented	11 (19%)	3 (5%)	45 (76%)
Motivational	2 (29%)	4 (57%)	1 (14%)
Conceptual	3 (75%)		1 (25%)
Explanatory	4 (33%)	2 (17%)	6 (50%)
Goal oriented	81 (49%)	38 (23%)	48 (28%)
Symptom oriented	11 (19%)	3 (5%)	45 (76%)
System oriented	9 (39%)	6 (26%)	8 (35%)
Total	101 (41%)	47 (19%)	101 (40%)

Examples were most frequently seen in the symptom oriented questions (81%). It was the easiest and most descriptive way of describing the error and presenting the solution. Similarly, 51% of the goal oriented questions included examples. However, the descriptions in the goal oriented questions were more general than the symptom oriented ones. Especially complex tasks were specified with general descriptions rather than specifics.

2.4. *Limitations of the data*

Although the Tcl newsgroup is a rich source of data about software inquiry episodes, the data collected is subject to some biases. Since most of the users in the newsgroup were programmers, the numbers of questions for different software engineering tasks were not equal. For example, there were no questions on software design activities, although there were some questions about design rationales. None of the posted questions were from the developers and maintainers of the Tcl/Tk system itself.

These limitations would be more serious if the objectives of the study were solely to observe and measure software inquiry behavior. However, the main objective here was to identify important question types, question topics, contextual factors, and answer content that might otherwise be overlooked. This objective was most definitely accomplished. But just because certain types of questions did not occur in large numbers in this sample set does not imply that they are insignificant. For example, questions relating to design rationale were not very common in this sample set, but there are solid independent grounds for supposing that design rationales are important things to document and explain.

The Internet provides other sources of software inquiry data which may provide relevant information. For example, there are many developer newsgroups where participants discuss bugs and propose new system features. We are beginning to examine some of these other data sets, to see if they provide further insights into how to design a system such as I-Doc.

2.5. *Implications for* I-Doc

The above study, along with previously articulated principles of good documentation (Mayhew, 1992), suggest a number of implications for the design of I-Doc. Some of these are already reflected in the current version of the system, others are the subject of current development.

1. *Organize around the users' tasks and goals.* The study shows that programmers' questions are predominantly goal oriented, just as novice users' questions are. This contrasts strongly with conventional system documentation, which is system oriented. I-Doc uses tasks and goals to organize presentations in the following ways. Tasks are represented explicitly at the macrotask level, and support for microtasks is being added as well. I-Doc's knowledge base can be extended by users, so as new tasks are identified they can be incorporated into the knowledge base. I-Doc's knowledge base thus grows along with the experience base of the users.

    Organizing the knowledge base around user goals poses challenges from a knowledge acquisition perspective. Conventional software development processes are oriented toward codifying properties of systems (e.g., requirements, design structures). They do not place much emphasis on describing how to perform particular software engineering tasks such as maintenance on those system. However, if code is well organized there is often a clear correspondence between user goals and system functions. For example, the user task of putting an image on a button may correspond to a particular procedure that paints images on buttons. I-Doc's knowledge base represents system functions and their mappings to domain concepts, in order to make it easier to map user goals onto system functions. It also represents intermediate design abstractions such as plans, so that delocalized plans can be mapped onto user goals as well.

2. *Focus presentation according to user task, especially for general questions.* Prior to performing the above study, we hypothesized that the same question might be answered in different ways, depending upon how the questioner described his or her task. The observed data did not strongly support this conjecture: if the questioner asked a specific question, it elicited a specific response, and there was relatively little scope for varying the response according to the user's task context. However, this leaves open the question of how user models might influence responses to general or imprecise questions. Questions that are input to information management systems such as I-Doc are often fragmentary and imprecise. The user may enter the name of a system function and ask for a description, without stating precisely what he or she wants to know about the system function. Requiring more precise questions imposes greater demands on the user to formulate the queries, and on the system to interpret the queries. Knowledge of user task enables I-Doc to restrict the information that it provides in response to imprecise queries, to avoid inundating the user with irrelevant information.

3. *Make presentations sensitive to user's expertise.* Explanations to novices tend to be briefer, and avoid making reference to other concepts that may be unfamiliar to the questioner. Although I-Doc explicitly models the user's expertise level, it does not yet make much use of this information when generating explanatory texts. However, the system has been designed specifically to take such user models into account. I-Doc incorporates a natural language generator for constructing phrases. The NL generator gives the system flexibility to express utterances in different ways, and sensitivity to user expertise is a key area where such flexibility is critical. Without this requirement, a simple template completion scheme for phrase generation would most likely suffice.

4. *Represent a wide range of concepts, and mappings between them.* This point has already been discussed in the context of mapping user goals onto code. Other mappings that were found to be important were relations between domain concepts and code. In Tcl/Tk these problems primarily among GUI developers who wanted to understand how to map concepts from the domain of user interfaces onto system concepts. We have found the problem to be even more acute in application software targeted to particular domains. In order to meet these requirements, it was necessary to provide I-Doc with an extensible representation scheme. We are still working on expanding the range of types of knowledge represented in I-Doc so that it corresponds more closely to the range of concerns observed in the empirical data, e.g., by including test cases, experience "war stories", etc.

3. I-Doc **system architecture**

We will now turn from discussion of the empirical studies that motivate I-Doc to the architecture of the system itself. The system has four major components: a *software repository*, *a documentation repository*, *Common Gateway Interface scripts*, and a *viewer*. The software repository contains software artifacts, and provides the information extracted from these artifacts. It responds to requests from both the CGI scripts and the documentation repository and returns the information required to answer the user's query. The documentation repository is a simple frame based knowledge base which is used to store two types of data. The first type is called *annotations* and contains the textual descriptions entered by the user for the software artifacts and for the user defined objects. The second type of data is the *presentation methods* that produce the documentation. These are included as part of the I-Doc system, can be extended by users and system administrators as needed. The CGI scripts use the presentation methods for retrieving information from the software and annotations repositories, and combines them to compose an HTML document which can then be viewed with a WWW client.

The viewer also accepts user queries and passes them to CGI scripts. Currently this is accomplished in two different ways. First I-Doc shows the user a list of hypertext links, each of which represents a different query likely to be asked at that point. The user then selects a link from the list. For example, one of the links might be labeled with the string "What are the platform dependencies?". By clicking on this link the user is able to obtain an answer to this question. The second way of entering a user query is by clicking on the "Query" button. The user is then presented with a text input field and can enter a question that is understandable by I-Doc. For example, when "What are the components of X?" is entered, I-Doc will first query the annotations and software repositories to resolve the name X. When it finds out what X is, it'll list the components of X to the user.

Figure 2 shows how the components described above organized and implemented. The software repository is currently built primarily on top of Software Refinery™. The program analysis tools **lex** and **yacc** are also employed to supply I-Doc with information about software. The repository consists primarily of annotated source code, together with pointers to other available documents. Representatives of other types of objects besides source code are also included. The system is currently designed to process Ada code, although some support is also being developed for other languages. Annotated source code was chosen as the primary information source because it is mechanically analyzable and is usually available for an implemented system. An interface process is used to transmit between the repository and the rest of the I-Doc system.

The documentation repository contains the annotations and methods used for producing the documentation. The current version is implemented in and built upon the Perl programming language. The data is stored in an SGML like format. It can be entered and modified by any text editor or using I-Doc's own editing capabilities. The information is organized around documentation objects which correspond either to software artifacts or other relevant concepts such as domain concepts, design abstractions, etc. Users can create new attributes and methods for the documentation objects as desired. The repository also has a simple inheritance capability which makes creating documentation templates

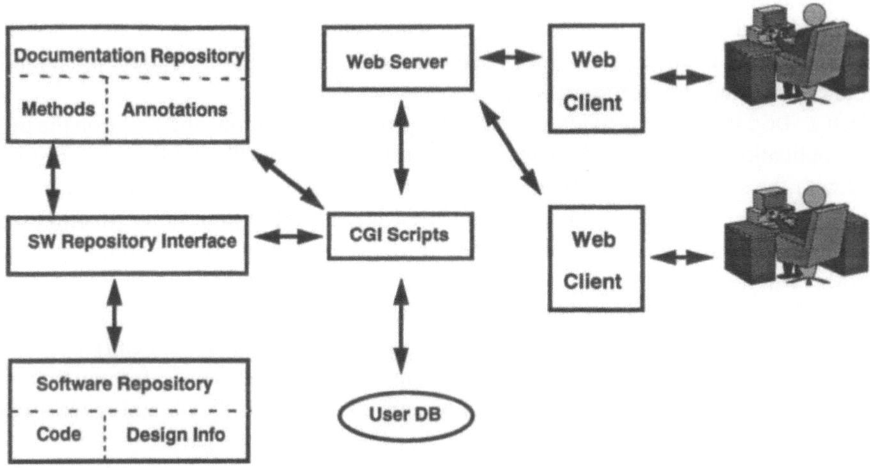

Figure 2. I-Doc system architecture.

easy. Organizations using I-Doc on software projects thus can create templates matching their own internal documentation standards, or can adjust I-Doc's tailored explanations to meet project-specific needs. Inheritable presentation methods can be used for implementing templates in I-Doc. Besides that, methods also provide extensibility to I-Doc by giving the user the ability to write access routines to new information sources. For example, if a company had a database of design records whose structure is not known apriori by I-Doc, they can write an access method for retrieving information from the database and use the design records in their documentation.

Presentation generation is built upon httpd, a common WWW server. httpd is usually employed at Web sites to transmit files to remote users. However, one can also use Common Gateway Interface of httpd to run programs that generate the information to be displayed, rather than to access a file. We have implemented a number of CGI scripts to be executed in this manner. The scripts access three information sources in order to generate presentations: the documentation repository, the software repository, and a database of information about each I-Doc user. httpd provides security and password protection to control access to the information.

To access I-Doc, one can use any Web client, although the preferred client configuration includes Netscape 2.0 and Java. The Web interface makes it easy for multiple members of a software project to obtain information about a common system, and reduces the need for special-purpose software. A demonstration version of the system is accessible via the Web addresses at the beginning of the paper.

4. Examples

The following example screen images illustrate how I-Doc works. The system documented here is Advanced Multi-Purpose Support Environment (AMPSE), a system developed by

TRW in Ada for the U.S. Air Force. This particular example was constructed from the Ada source code and corresponding design documents, which were annotated and cross-linked by hand. Editing facilities have since been built which enable I-Doc users to create such annotated knowledge bases themselves.

Each I-Doc user must provide some simple profile information: their role on the project (e.g., application programmer, maintainer, etc.), their macrotask, and their level of familiarity with the system. In this example, the user has selected Application Programmer as the role, Interface to System as the task, and High as the level of familiarity. In other words, the user has an understanding of what AMPSE does, and is building an application which interface with it.

Figure 3 shows an overview of the system, from the designed perspective. The description is a combination of dynamically generated structured text and dynamically constructed hyperlinks. The objective is always to provide a manageable amount of information relevant to the user's question. Two types of hyperlinks are shown: links for obtaining elaborations

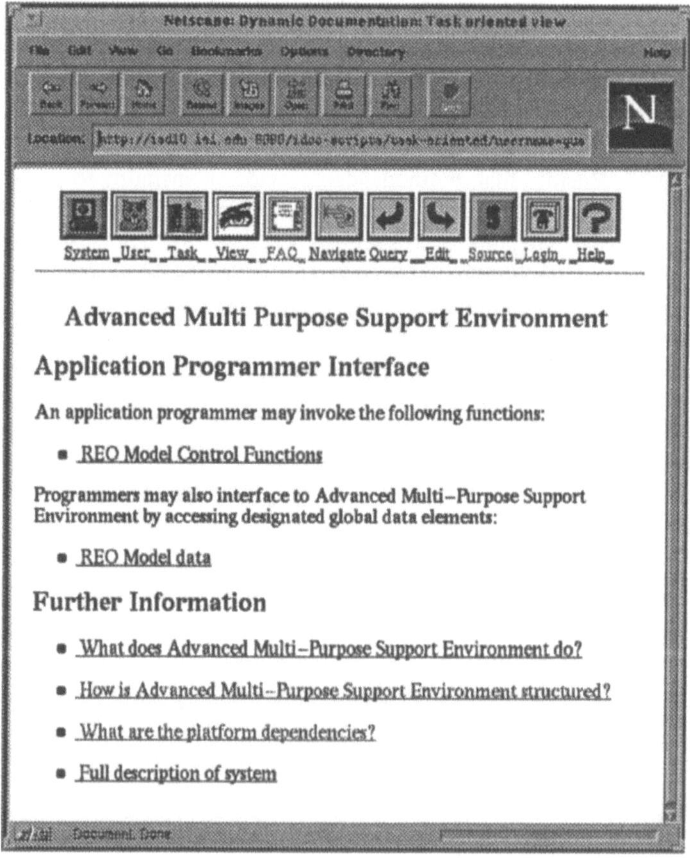

Figure 3.   **High-level description of the AMPSE system.**

on the information presented, and links for obtaining answers to other questions. An example elaboration link is the link labeled "REO Model Control Function", which provides information about procedures that external applications are expected to invoke. An example question link is the one labeled "What are the platform dependencies?" When this link is selected, available information about platform dependencies is provided. Such links are needed in case information that the presentation generator filtered out is in fact of interest to the user.

Figure 4 shows what results if the information is not filtered using the user model. All attributes of the system are then shown, only some of which fit on the screen shown.

Descriptions can be similarly obtained for various objects and concepts associated with a system. One may also view the actual source code using the hypertext interface, as shown in figure 5. Declared symbols in the text appear as hypertext links; by traversing these links one can obtain information about the corresponding symbols.

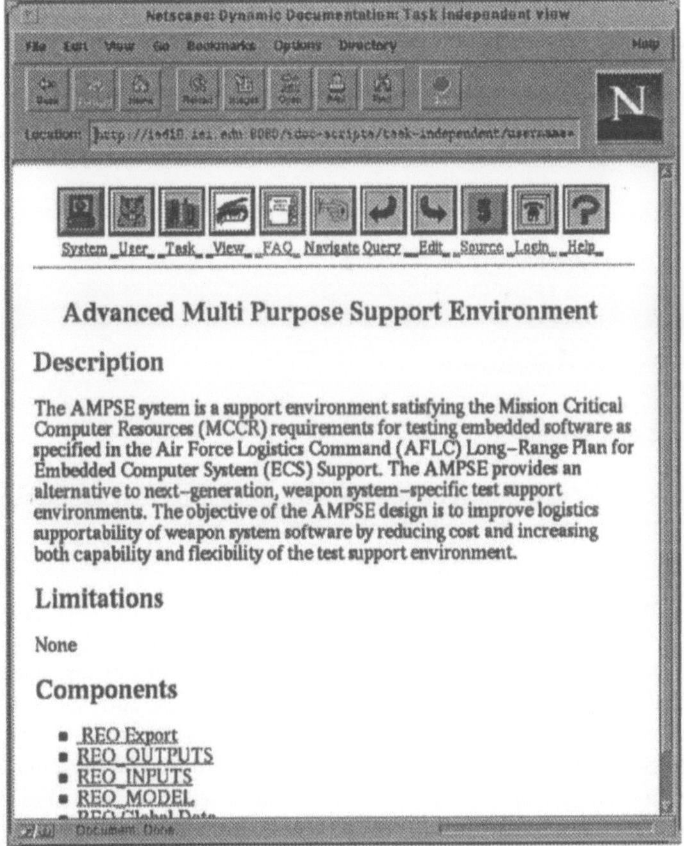

Figure 4.   A non-task-oriented view.

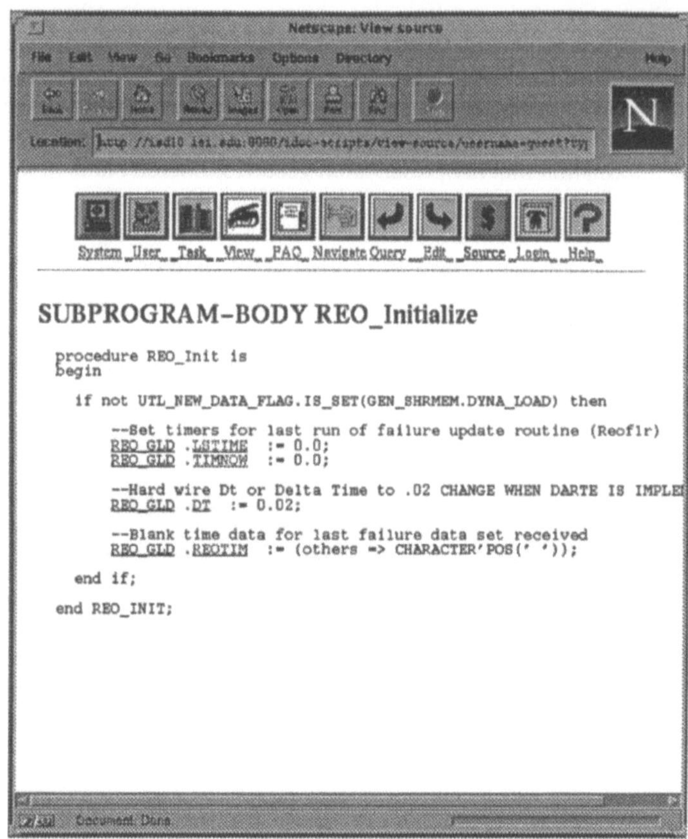

Figure 5.   A hypertext view of program code.

5.   Underlying mechanisms

The following is a brief description of the representations and inference mechanisms used in the I-Doc software repository, and the presentation generation.

5.1.   *Software repository mechanisms*

Conceptually, the software repository is simply a collection of objects, each with a set of attributes and relationships with other objects. Some objects correspond to individual program components, and are represented internally using Software Refinery's parse tree representation. Some objects contain information from multiple program components. For example, in Ada each package has a specification and a separate body. For presentation purposes, however, the package may be treated as a single object, whose properties are obtained from both the specification and the body. Other objects do not correspond to any program component at all, in which case a separate frame representation is used. The repository manages this heterogeneous representation so that the presentation generator need not be concerned with the internal representations employed.

Each link from a parse tree node to its immediate subtrees is accessible as an attribute of the parse tree object, as is the link from the node to its parent. Each parse tree link that associates named program objects is also treated as a specialization of an abstract **component** relation. This provides a language-independent way for the I-Doc presentation system to access program substructures. Definition-use relations, derived from the Software Refinery symbol table, are also treated as attributes. Additionally, each object has a "source text" attribute, which consists of program text in which each symbol reference has been annotated with SGML markup tags, which indicate where the symbol definition can be found. This marked up source text is used to generated hypertext versions of source code such as that shown in figure 5.

The repository also performs automated processing on object attributes. Some attributes are computed from more primitive attributes; some are defeasibly inherited from the attributes of other objects. For example, the attributes of an Ada procedure body may be derived from attributes of the corresponding procedure specification or from the package specification containing it. This capability is similar to the relation derivation mechanisms incorporated in the ARIES system (Johnson et al., 1992), although limited in that no provision exists as of yet for editing derived attributes.

5.2. *Documentation repository*

Documentation repository is a simple frame based knowledge base where attributes and methods of software and user defined objects are stored. Data is stored in an SGML like format. Figure 6 is an example documentation repository with 3 object definitions. Each object definition is placed within <<OBJECT>> and <</OBJECT>> tags. The first line after the <<OBJECT>> tag is the object key and consists of the concatenation of the name of the system, object type and object name. For example, the second object entry is AMPSE.Package.Main which contains the attributes of the Main package of AMPSE system. The last object AMPSE.User.Process is a user defined object and contains the attributes of the AMPSE process model. "User defined objects" are objects which have no corresponding artifact in the software repository. Such objects are used to represent the wide range of concepts found in the empirical study to be relevant to software explanation: architectural abstractions, domain concepts, etc.

A '-' stands for the default object at a given level. The first object in the figure AMPSE.Package.- contains the default attributes for all package objects. When an attribute of an object needs to be resolved during program execution, I-Doc first tries to find whether there is an explicit description of that object attribute. If not, it will use the default attributes for that object type. If no default attributes for that object type are found, the defaults for the system are inherited. This inheritance mechanism simplifies the documentation generation process, since default attributes for objects can be provided. This feature makes defining documentation templates easy and provides compact storage of the information. Although the documentation templates could be defined as user defined objects and called in the presentation methods, without inheritance it is not possible to use a template for a class of objects.

```
<<OBJECT>>
AMPSE.Package.
<<PRESENTATION>>
print "<CENTER><H2>Package $unit</H2></CENTER>"
print "<H3>Author</H3>";
print &get_package_author($unit);
if ($annotations{$key."!USER!WHAT"}) {
    print "<H3>Description</H3>";
    print $annotations{$key."!USER!WHAT"};
}else {
    print "No description is available for this package<P>";
}
<</PRESENTATION>>
<<OBJECT>>

<<OBJECT>>
AMPSE.Package.Main
<<USER>>
<<WHAT>>
The AMPSE system is a support environment satisfying the Mission Critical Computer
Resources (MCCR) requirements for testing embedded software as specified in the Air
Force Logistics Command (AFLC) Long-Range Plan for Embedded Computer System (ECS)
Support. The AMPSE provides an alternative to next-generation,.......
For more information, please check
<A HREF="http://www.isi.edu/isd/i-doc.html> I-Doc homepage</A>
<</WHAT>>
<</USER>>
<</OBJECT>>

<<OBJECT>>
AMPSE.User.Process
<</OBJECT>>
```

Figure 6.   Simplified example of part of the AMPSE documentation repository.

Attributes themselves are also stored within tags. Users can define new objects and add attributes to existing objects. Attributes contain strings which can be text, variables or Perl programs. One of the attributes, PRESENTATION, has a special meaning and is used for producing the documentation page for the object. Users can embed links to web documents, call special access methods to external information sources and do anything possible to do with Perl programming language in defining attributes. As an example, let's look at how the documentation for the Main package is generated.

When the user requests documentation for the Main package, I-Doc first tries to find a presentation attribute for AMPSE.Package.Main object. Since no presentation attribute is specified for this particular object, the presentation attribute of AMPSE.Package.- will be used. Evaluating the presentation attribute in Perl will yield part of the HTML output that will produce the documentation page on the Web viewer. The user can use variables (e.g., $unit is a system variable and refers to the current object name),object attributes (e.g., $annotations { $key."!USER!WHAT"} refers to the WHAT attribute of AMPSE.Package.Main object, i.e., the string "The AMPSE system...") or a method (e.g., &get_package_author method will return the author's name given the package name). The user can define new methods, or use existing ones. Task oriented documentation is also generated via such special presentation methods.

Users are not required to know Perl or the structure of the documentation repository in order to use I-Doc. I-Doc creates a default documentation repository for new projects when they are defined. Users do not need to make any additions or changes to this initial repository, if they are satisfied with the documentation. They need to learn Perl and the structure of the documentation repository only when they want to tailor I-Doc to their needs. We believe most users will need special methods to access external data sources like design records, test reports etc. I-Doc is designed to be an extensible, open system and gives the users the ability to tailor the system to their needs.

5.3.   User database

I-Doc currently records for each user the following information:

- what system they are currently working on,
- their role in the system development project (e.g., user, maintainer, etc.),
- their current macrotask,
- some parameters indicating their degree of expertise, and
- their individual preferences regarding the form of the output.

Expertise is classified qualitatively as novice, intermediate, and expert, in each of several topic categories: the implementation language of the system (e.g., Ada), the application domain, and the implementation platform. Currently only one individual preference is recorded: whether the user prefers brief explanations or detailed explanations.

The user database parameters are assigned to special variables within the presentation scripts. Presentations can be customized for particular user characteristics by having the presentation methods test the user parameters. At present the user parameters must be set explicitly by the user via special forms, and remain fixed until the forms are explicitly changed by the user. We have been considering two ways of reducing this burden on the user. If the user is employing a software process support tool that has some model of the user tasks, we would like to input this information directly from the process tool. This would allow I-Doc to track user tasks more automatically. Secondly, requests for follow-on explanations and elaborations could be used as evidence that the user model is inaccurate, so that the model can be automatically changed.

5.4.   CGI scripts

Presentations are generated by scripts written in the Perl language (Wall and Schwartz, 1991). Perl was chosen because it is a high-level language somewhat comparable to Lisp,

```
<HEAD><TITLE>Dynamic Documentation: Task independent view</TITLE></HEAD>
<BODY BGCOLOR="#EEFFF8"#TEXT="#000000"#LINK="#CC0000"#VLINK="#000055">
<CENTER>
<a href="http://lt.isi.edu/idoc-scripts/select-system/username=guest?
type=Module&unit=__Main__&version=0&id=0">
<img src="http://lt.isi.edu/button-system.gif"></a>
```

. . . HTML output for the rest of the button descriptions is deleted for brevity

```
<FONT SIZE=-1>
<a href="http://lt.isi.edu/idoc-scripts/select-system/username=guest?
type=Module&unit=__Main__&version=0id=0">System</a>
```

. . . HTML output for the rest of the button lables is deleted for brevity

```
</CENTER> </FONT>
<HR>
<CENTER><H1>Advanced Multi Purpose Support Environment</H1></CENTER>
<H3>Description</H3>
The AMPSE system is a support environment satisfying the Mission
Critical Computer Resources (MCCR) requirements for testing embedded
software as specified in the Air Force Logistics Command (AFLC)
Long-Range plan for Embedded Computer System (ECS)
Support. The AMPSE provides in alternative to next-generation, weapon
system-specific test support environments. The objective of the AMPSE
design is to improve logistics supportability of weapon system
software by reducing cost and increasing both capability and
flexibility of the test support environment.
<H3>Limitations</H3>
None
<H3>Components</H3>
<UL>
<LI><a href="http://lt.isi.edu/idoc-scripts/task-oriented/username=guest?
      type=MODULE&unit=REO_Export&version=1&id=20"> REO_Export</a>
<LI><a href="http://lt.isi.edu/idoc-scripts/task-oriented/username=guest?
      type=MODULE&unit=REO_OUTPUTS&version=1&id=21"> REO_OUTPUTS</a>
<LI><a href="http://lt.isi.edu/idoc-scripts/task-oriented/username=guest?
      type=MODULE&unit=REO_INPUTS&version=1&id=22"> REO_INPUTS</a>
<LI><a href="http://lt.isi.edu/idoc-scripts/task-oriented/username=guest?
      type=MODULE&unit=REO_MODEL&version=1&id=23"> REO_MODEL</a>
<LI><a href="http://lt.isi.edu/idoc-scripts/task-oriented/username=guest?
      type=PACKAGE-SPECIFICATION&unit=REO_Global_Data&version=1&id=0">
REO Global Data</a>
<LI><a href="http://lt.isi.edu/idoc-scripts/task-oriented/username=guest?
      type=SUPERPROGRAM-BODY&unit=REO_Image&version=1&id=0"> REO Image</a>
</UL></BODY>
```

Figure 7.   HTML output for non task oriented view example.

has strong string manipulations facilities, but does not produce large binary files. The scripts can be executed on demand by the `httpd` server, without delays for system initialization as in Lisp.

Each script is supplied five parameters. The first one, `username`, identifies the user making the request. The remaining parameters identify the object to be described. The parameters are embedded in the WWW addresses (URLs) for the hypertext links. For example the URL for the REO_Export link in figure 4 contains the following script invocation:

`"task-independent/username = guest?type = MODULE&unit = REO_Export &version=1&id=12"`.

`task-independent` is the name of CGI script that produces task independent documentation. The parameters follow the CGI script name and are as follows: "guest" is the name of the current user, module is the software object type and `REO_Export` is the name of the object. The version and id parameters are values assigned by the software repository to distinguish the object from others of the same name and type. Each script is responsible for generating URLs for follow-up questions and associating them with hypertext links in the generated page.

Presentation generation occurs in the following phases. First, the script retrieves the user attributes from the user database. After that, the presentation method is resolved by using the documentation repository. If the object name is not specified in the repository, then the inheritance mechanism will be used. Although each object can possibly have its own presentation attribute, most of the objects use one of the default presentation methods. After the presentation method is found, it is executed to determine the content and the format of the documentation. Depending upon the current values of user parameters, the presentation method may invoke additional task-dependent and/or expertise-dependent presentation methods for fleshing out the presentation details.

The presentation methods query the software and the annotations repository for this information. For example, in figure 4 the description comes from the annotations repository and the component information is retrieved from the software repository. The description is formatted as a text block whereas the components are formatted as a list of items. The methods also convert the information into HyperText Markup Language (HTML) which can then be transmitted and viewed by a WWW client. Figure 7 shows the HTML output from the CGI script used to generate the text shown in figure 4; it contains several examples of `I-Doc` invocations embedded in hypertext links.

6. Extensions and future work

Since the repository mechanisms is `I-Doc` can be readily extended by defining new object categories and attributes, there are no fundamental limitations in the kinds of information content that can be captured. Likewise, there are no limitations to the kinds of explanations that can be generated. However, the amount of effort required to apply `I-Doc` to any given software system can vary considerably. We are currently extending the system in order to reduce the amount of effort required.

In order for `I-Doc` to explain software effectively, several kinds of information are required: information about the problem domain, requirements and implementation constraints, architecture and design structures, code structures, examples and test cases, etc. Knowledge acquisition is thus a serious issue, especially for legacy systems where relevant information sources may be unavailable or out of date.

The knowledge acquistion problem is addressed in part by interfacing to analysis tools that are able to supply the necessary information. Code analysis tools are especially relevant in this regard. Publically available tools such as Bison are currently being employed to extend the set of languages that I-Doc can support. We are also evaluating other code analysis tools to determine how they might be interfaced to I-Doc.

Domain and requirements information typically must be obtained from informal textual documents. I-Doc has therefore been extended to with an analyzer for extracting relevant concepts in textual documents. The analyzer sorts through the text looking for recurring words and phrases. It presents the list of phrases to the I-Doc user. The user can then select meaningful phrases from the list. I-Doc then automatically creates objects in the documentation repository corresponding to the selected phrases, and links them to their occurrences in the original document. We plan to create additional analyzers for specific types of structured documents such as requirements documents.

In order to make most effective use of the acquired information, it is important to be able to organize concepts into hierarchies, and to define new concepts in terms of other concepts. The LOOM knowledge representation system is being introduced into I-Doc to help achieve these purposes. LOOM can also be used to define patterns which can be matched against the software repository. This provides a limited code analysis capability that can be used directly within I-Doc, and reduces the need to invoke external analysis tools.

Additional extensions to I-Doc are underway, or are planned for the near future. For example, we have incorporated Elhadad's FUG natural language generator (McKeown and Elhadad, 1991), and are working to make more extensive use of this generator in producing explanations. Automated word selection, focus and text organization capabilities, which require the use of a text generator, are important in tailoring the documentation to the user.

We had made a start at incorporating dynamically generated diagrams into I-Doc. A Java applet has been developed for drawing decomposition diagrams based on high-level descriptions including lists of nodes and edges. Future work will make use of this and similar capabilities to generate tailored diagrams emphasizing aspects of the system of interest to the user. Ultimately it will be possible to integrate diagrams and text in order to explain software more effectively.

Meanwhile further empirical studies of software inquiries will be conducted. We need to understand the relation between the user questions and task better. However, it is not easy to capture this relation for all tasks. That's why we are considering building the analysis process itself into I-Doc. Once we define methods to answer the basic user questions, it won't be hard to get feedback from the user and tailor the documentation further. Besides, the user can define new tasks and by analyzing his question pattern for those tasks, an association between the task and the question types can be made.

Finally, examples are very important in understanding the questions and presenting the answers. We are planning to study the examples further and try to generate situation specific examples in the documentation.

7. Conclusion

This paper has described efforts to analyze the inquiry process that is central to software understanding, and to build a tool which provides automated support for this inquiry process. Software understanding thus becomes less search oriented, and more like a question-answer dialog.

The components of the system are currently undergoing trial evaluation. Groups outside of USC/ISI have expressed interest in using I-Doc for their own projects, and plans are in place for providing them with the system for their own use. Results from these evaluations should be available by the time this paper goes to press.

Acknowledgments

I-Doc project members Rogelio Adobbati and Amy Biermann contributed to the system functionality described in this paper. The authors wish to thank Wright Laboratory for providing the software examples used in this paper. This work is sponsored by the Advanced Research Projects Agency and administered by Wright Laboratory, Air Force Material Command, under Contract No. F33615-91-1-1402.

References

Brooks, R. 1983. Towards a theory of the comprehension of computer programs. *International Journal of Man-Machine Studies*, 18:543–554.

Corbi, T.A. 1990. Program understanding: Challenge for the 1990s. *IBM Systems Journal*, 28(2):294–306.

Herbsleb, J.D. and Kuwana, E. 1993. Preserving knowledge in design projects: What designers need to know. In *INTERCHI'93*.

Hill, W.C. and Miller, J.R. 1988. Justified advice: A semi-naturalistic study of advisory strategies. In *CHI'88*. ACM.

Hunsaker, P.L., Coffey, R.E., and Cook, C.W. 1994. *Management and Organizational Behavior*. Austen Press.

Johnson, W.L., Feather, M.S., and Harris, D.R. 1992. Representation and presentation of requirements knowledge. *IEEE Trans. on Software Engineering*, 18(10):853–869.

Lakhotia, A. 1993. Understanding someone else's code: Analysis of experiences. *Journal of Systems Software*, 2:93–100.

Lazonder, A.W. and van der Meij, J. 1993. The minimal manual: Is less really more? *Int. J Man-Machine Studies*, 39:729–752.

Mayhew, D. 1992. *Principles & Guidelines in Software User Interface Design*. Prentice Hall.

McKeown, K.R. and Elhadad, M. 1991. *A Contrastive Evaluation of Functional Unification Grammar for Surface Language Generation: A Case Study in the Choice of Connectives*, Kluwer Academic Publishers, Norwell, MA, pp. 351–392.

Moore, J.D. 1995. *Participating in Explanatory Dialogues*. MIT Press, Cambridge, MA.

Rajlich, V., Doran, J., and Gudla, R.T.S. 1994. Layered explanation of software: A methodology for program comprehension. In *Proceedings of the Workshop on Program Comprehension*.

Selfridge, P.G. 1990. Integrating code knowledge with a software information system. In *Proceedings of the 5th Annual Knowledge-Based Software Assistant Conference*, Syracuse, NY, pp. 183–195.

Soloway, E., Pinto, J., Letovsky, S.I., Littman, D., and Lampert, R. 1988. Designing documentation to compensate for delocalized plans. *Communications of the ACM*, 31(11).

Wall, L. and Schwartz, R.L. 1991. *Programming perl*. O'Reilly & Associates, Sebastopol, CA.

Wright, P. 1988. Issue of content and presentation in document design. In M. Helander, editor, *Handbook of Human-Computer Interaction*, Elsevier Science Publishers B.V. (North Holland), Chap. 28, pp. 629–652.

Automated Software Engineering, 4, 77–106 (1997)

Test Case Generation as an AI Planning Problem

ADELE E. HOWE   howe@cs.colostate.edu

ANNELIESE VON MAYRHAUSER   avm@cs.colostate.edu
Computer Science Department, Colorado State University, Fort Collins, CO 80523

RICHARD T. MRAZ   mraz@cs.usafa.af.mil
HQ USAFA/DFCS, 2354 Fairchild Hall, Suite 6K41, U.S. Air Force Academy, CO 80840

Abstract. While Artificial Intelligence techniques have been applied to a variety of software engineering applications, the area of automated software testing remains largely unexplored. Yet, test cases for certain types of systems (e.g., those with command language interfaces and transaction based systems) are similar to plans. We have exploited this similarity by constructing an automated test case generator with an AI planning system at its core. We compared the functionality and output of two systems, one based on Software Engineering techniques and the other on planning, for a real application: the StorageTek robot tape library command language. From this, we showed that AI planning is a viable technique for test case generation and that the two approaches are complementary in their capabilities.

Keywords: System testing, AI planning, blackbox testing

1. Automated Test Case Generation

Testing consumes a large amount of time and effort in software development. Although critical for ensuring reliability and satisfaction, much of the process is tedious: constructing data sets and/or sequences of commands to probe for faults. Some of the test cases will uncover faults, but one expects that most will not. A variety of approaches have been put forth for automated test generation in Software Engineering (SE) (see section 2).

Another approach is to acknowledge a similarity between some types of test cases (i.e., sequences of commands for software with command language interfaces) and plans in Artificial Intelligence (AI). Both are sequences of commands to achieve some goal; both need to conform to syntactic requirements of the commands and the semantic interactions between commands. Considerable research in AI planning has addressed subgoal and operator interactions; thus, the mechanisms of planning seem ideally suited to test case generation. In this paper, we explore the similarities between test case and plan generation, propose another approach, as implemented in a prototype, to automated test case generation using an AI planner and compare the new approach to an existing SE approach.

We selected the SE approach for comparison with two criteria in mind: First, the approach should be applicable to system testing and represent knowledge about the application at the system level. Second, the generation method must have been successful in practice as evidenced by at least a field study. Although our prototype might be small and limited in capabilities, testing it against a real application is crucial to heading off concerns about AI only being applicable to "toy problems".

These two criteria directed us to select Application Domain Based Testing (ADBT) (von Mayrhauser et al., 1994c, von Mayrhauser et al., 1994d) and its test generation tool *Sleuth*. They support system testing of applications by building a model of the application domain which is used in the associated tool *Sleuth* to customize a test generation engine. Test generation is black box and is for user interfaces represented by a command language, or for transaction or request based systems. These characteristics fulfill our first selection criterion.

Application Domain Based Testing also fulfills the second criterion. Storage Technology Corp. has done a field study on the test generation method's usefulness (Figliulo et al., 1996). An experienced tester tested two major product releases, one with and one without using *Sleuth* over a full 12 week test cycle. The amount of new code and the development process were comparable. The test cycle without *Sleuth* uncovered 38 incidents, using *Sleuth* produced 135 incidents. Further, the post-release incident rate was 30% lower for the version tested with *Sleuth*.

2. Background on Testing

For systems with a command language interface, system tests consist of sequences of commands to test the system for correct behavior. Similarly, transaction based or request oriented systems can be tested by generating transactions or requests. Traditionally, test automation for both command language and transaction based systems is based on a variety of grammars or state machine representations.

Automated test generation for systems with a command language interface represents each command using a grammar, generates commands from the grammar, and runs the list of commands as the test case (for early work see (Purdom, 1972, Bauer and Finger, 1979)). When using grammars for test case generation, we also need to address command language semantics (Bazzichi and Spadafora, 1982), (Celentano et al., 1980), (Duncanc and Hutchison, 1981), (Ince, 1987).
(Duncan and Hutchison, 1981), (von Mayrhauser and Crawford-Hines, 1993) used attribute grammars for test case generation. The syntax and semantics of the command language were encoded as grammar productions. Test case generation is a single stage algorithm. This encoding poses difficulties (von Mayrhauser et al., 1994c); not the least of which is that for the average system tester these grammars are difficult to write and maintain and that the generation process does not follow the test engineers' thought processes, particularly in terms of testing goals and refinement of these goals at successive levels of abstraction.

Transaction based systems and state transition aspects of some other systems have been tested using state machine representations (Chow, 1977, Fujiwara et al., 1991). State machine representations work well for generating sensible sequences of command types, but become cumbersome for generation of both sequencing as well as command details of systems with large and intricate command languages.

Automatic generation, whether based on grammars or state machines, requires making choices during the traversal of the representations. The choices are due to ambiguities as well as the purposeful inclusion of options in the representation. Choice is directed by incorporating selection rules of various types. (Purdom, 1972) integrates "coverage rules" for grammar productions to reduce choice, while Maurer (Maurer, 1990) uses probabilistic context free grammars that are enhanced by selection rules including permutations, combinations, dynamic probabilities, and Poisson distribution. Thus, value selection is based on making choices relating to the representation of the command language or state machine.

Alternatively, one can argue that choices should be made depending on the functional characteristics of the system. Functional testing according to (Myers, 1979) uses heuristic criteria related to the requirements. (Goodenough and Gerhart, 1975) suggest partitioning the input domain into equivalence classes and selecting test data from each class. Category-partition testing (Ostrand and Balcer, 1988) accomplishes this by analyzing the specification, identifying separately testable functional units, categorizing each function's input, and finally partitioning categories into equivalence classes. (Richardson et al., 1989) considers these approaches manual, leaving test case selection completely to the tester through document reading activities. Further, partition-testing as a testing criterion does not guarantee that tests will actually uncover faults (Hamlet and Taylor, 1990, Tsoulakas et al., 1993, Weyuker, 1991). From a practical standpoint, a better approach is to combine different test generation methods with a variety of testing criteria. Examples are to combine exhaustive generation of some commands or parameter values with probabilistic or combinatorial criteria for others, which requires flexible command generation methods.

(von Mayrhauser and Crawford-Hines, 1993, von Mayrhauser et al., 1994c), (von Mayrhauser et al., 1994d) developed a test generation method, Application Domain Based Testing, that addresses the need of software testers for a tool that supports their thought processes. Test generation addresses three levels of abstraction: the process level (i.e., how the target software commands are put together into scripts to achieve high level tasks), the command level (i.e., which specific commands are included in the scripts), and the parameter level (i.e., particular parameter values used in command templates). Each level has its own generation rules that represent syntax and semantics at that level. Definition of content of rules at each level is the result of a specialized application domain analysis. The resulting domain model forms the basis for test case generation.

So far, few approaches to software testing use artificial intelligence methods. (Deason et al., 1991) uses a rule-based system to test programs. The rules reflect white box criteria and use information about control flow and data flow of the code. To apply this method to system testing would require an entirely new set of rules. (Chilenski and Newcomb, 1994) use a resolution-refutation theorem prover to determine structural test coverage and coverage feasibility. Again, this aids white box testing, rather than system testing. (Zeil and Wild, 1993) describe a method for refining test case descriptions into actual test cases by imposing additional constraints and using a knowledge base to describe entities, their refinements, and relationships between them. This is considered useful for test criteria that yield a set of test case descriptors which require further processing before usable test data can be achieved.

(Anderson et al., 1995) use neural networks as classifiers to predict which test cases are likely to reveal faults. Automated test case generation can easily generate tens of thousands of tests, particularly when random or grammar based methods are chosen. Running them takes time. After a subset has been run, results indicate whether or not the test revealed a fault. The neural net is trained on test case measurements as inputs and test results (severity of failure) as output. This is then used to filter out test cases that are not likely to find problems. While the study is preliminary, the results are very encouraging for guiding and focusing testing, making it more efficient and effective.

3. AI Planning for Testing

Test cases are *sequences* of operations where the order matters. Operations may be executed only in particular contexts or in particular orders. Thus, coordinating the inclusion of operations and their interactions is a source of complexity in test case generation. Fortunately, representing and reconciling operation interactions is the purpose of most AI planning systems.

Roughly speaking, to generate a plan, a planning system is given: (1) a description of the operators, (2) an initial state of the world and (3) a goal state. Operator descriptions have parameters (i.e., what objects are involved in the operator), preconditions (i.e., what must be the case to use this operator) and effects (i.e., what happens to the system after the operator is executed).

Many classical or deliberative planning systems generate a plan by in effect proving that a sequence of actions will transform the initial state into the goal state. Planning works as follows: pick a goal to achieve, find an operator whose effects include the goal, add the preconditions of the operator to the list of goals to achieve and repeat the three steps until no goals remain unresolved or all unresolved goals are satisfied by the initial state.

What makes planning an attractive paradigm for software testing is the similarity of plans to programs and its emphasis on goals. From its early days, planning was thought of as a type of automatic programming (Sussman, 1973); the form of a plan and a test case can be made to be extremely similar. Unlike programs, plans do not always include control structures and new plans often must be generated for each test case.

The emphasis on goals means that sequences of actions (e.g., plans or test cases) are generated specifically to fulfill some purpose and that it is relatively easy to generate different plans for different goals. So, instead of focusing on *what* cases to generate, we think about *why* we wish to test certain aspects of the system and let the planning system determine *what* cases to generate. This appears to complement a goal oriented testing approach by human testers who start thinking about *what* they want to test before deciding *how* they will do so. Traditional generation methods are procedural, emphasizing how generation has to proceed.

Planning has been used for a variety of applications within software engineering. For example, Anderson and Fickas used planning as the underlying representation for software requirements and specification (Fickas and Anderson, 1988, Anderson, 1993). The planner automates portions of the requirements engineering process: proposing a functional specification, critiquing the specification and modifying the specification to remove deficiencies. Another system, Critter, assisted analysts in designing composite systems (Fickas and Helm, 1992) by viewing the design of composite systems as problem solving. The system included tools for generating example plans/scenarios that violate problem constraints (a specific type of design test case), simulating portions of the design and expediting design decision making and evaluation.

Huff has exploited the structure of plans and their ability to relate disparate goals in several applications in software engineering, e.g., (Huff88) in process engineering and (Huff, 1992) in software adaptation. Rist represented different levels of functionality and goals in programs using a plan representation (Rist, 1992); his PARE system extracted the abstract plan structure from PASCAL programs to aid in program design and re-use.

3.1. *The Planning System for the Prototype*

We used the UCPOP 2.0 planner as the basis for our prototype test case generator (Barrett et al., 1993, Penberthy and Weld, 1992). The planner was selected because it is relatively easy to use and the software is easily obtained. UCPOP is a "Universal Conditional Partial Order Planner" which means that it can represent goals that include universal quantifiers (e.g., execute some operation on *all* possible objects) and that it does not order the sequence of operators in the plan until necessary, which makes it more flexible.

The planner requires a domain knowledge base of operators. Operators are represented in structures and are described in terms of their parameters, preconditions, and effects. Parameters in the operators refer to all of the objects appearing in the action description and are included in the preconditions and effects. Preconditions describe any state information that makes an operator eligible to be executed, and effects describe how state is changed by an operator.

As with many other planners, UCPOP builds a plan by incrementally adding actions that reduce the difference between the initial state and the goal state. To support that process, the domain description should be complete: include all effects and preconditions of all known operators. If it is incomplete or incorrect, the plan may be as well. Rules about which operator to apply are mostly handled by the planning system's manipulation of the operators, but may be tuned through the use of search control rules that direct selection of goals and operators.

4. Experimental Domain: StorageTek Robot Tape Library Command Language

Storage Technology Corporation (**StorageTek**) produces an Automated Cartridge System (ACS) that stores and retrieves cartridge tapes (StorageTek, 1992). The system maintains magnetic tape cartridges in a 12-sided "silo" called a Library Storage Module (LSM). Each LSM contains a vision-assisted robot and storage for up to 6000 cartridges. Tapes occupy cells in the panels. New tapes are entered through a special door called a Cartridge Access Port (CAP). Figure 1 shows a single LSM with tape drives, access port, and control unit. The robot inside the LSM identifies tapes using an optical scanner. Once a tape is identified, the robot moves the tape to a cell, mounts the tape in a tape drive, dismounts the tape, or ejects the tape through a CAP. One ACS can support up to sixteen LSMs. Figure 2 shows a "top-down" look at an ACS with three LSMs. Tapes move between LSMs through special doors called "pass-through-ports."

The ACS and its components are controlled through a command language interface called the *Host Software Component* (HSC). Each HSC supports from one to sixteen ACS systems.

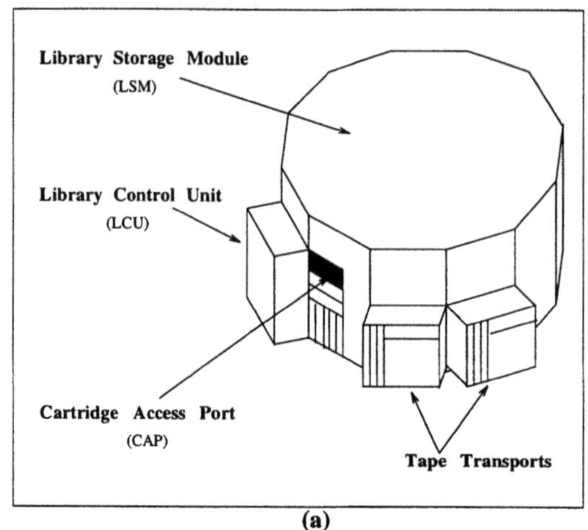

Figure 1. Library Storage Module (StorageTek, 1992)

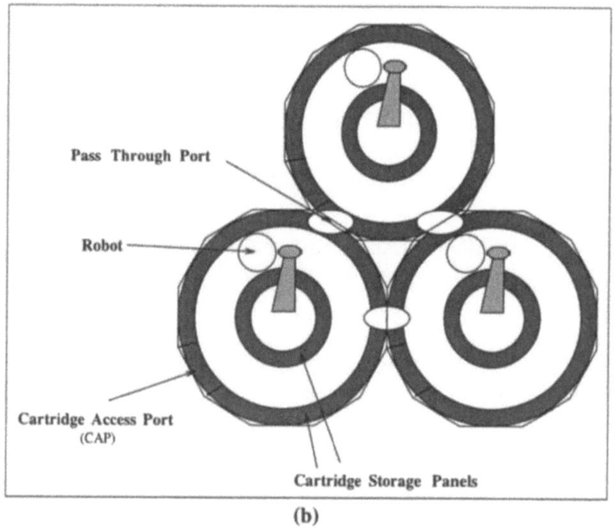

Figure 2. Automated Cartridge System with Three LSMs (StorageTek, 1992)

HSC commands manipulate cartridges, set the status of various components in the system, and display status information to the operator's console. The command language consists of 30 commands and 45 parameters.

The experimental subdomain uses 9 commands and 11 parameters. The subdomain models "Moving" tapes within the ACS and "Mounting/Dismounting" tapes to/from tape drives. We chose this subdomain because it captures all the sophisticated aspects of the

Table 1. Domain Analysis Steps for Domain Based Testing

Domain Analysis Step	Domain Model Component
1. Object Analysis	
1.1. Define Objects and Object Elements	Set of Objects
1.2. Define Default Parameter Values and	Default Parameter Sets
Object/Object Element Glossaries	
1.3. Define Object Hierarchy	Object Hierarchy
1.4. Annotate Hierarchy with Parameter Constraints	Parameter Constraint Rules
2. Command Definition	
2.1. Command Language Representation	Command Language Syntax
2.2. Identify Pre/Post Conditions	
2.3. Identify Intracommand Rules	Intracommand Rules
3. Script Definition (Command Sequencing)	
3.1. Script Class Definition	Script Classes
3.2. Script Rule Definition	Command Sequencing Rules

application while stripping from it several simple commands (involving command name and one or two possible parameter values) and those commands that are not part of behavioral rules. This gives the subdomain the realism of the application, without all the bulk.

5. Domain Analysis

Domain analysis is well known in the reuse community (Hooper and Chester, 1991, Biggerstaff and Perlis, 1989). Here we apply it to build an application domain model from which to generate test cases. Thus our domain analysis is specialized due to its purpose: testing the application. In addition to domain components that are command language independent, we also need to capture the syntax of the command language. The representation should be such that no syntax independent changes are necessary when changing command languages (e.g., when comparing Storage Technology's versus IBM's versions of robot-controlled tape libraries).

Table 1 lists the steps for the domain analysis and the domain model components generated at each step. The next subsections describe details of applying this analysis (von Mayrhauser et al., 1994c). We will use the **StorageTek** automated tape library to illustrate each step.

5.1. *Object analysis*

The first step identifies the *objects* of the system, *object elements*, and *relationships* between the objects. *Objects* denote physical or logical entities from the problem domain. *Object elements* define qualities and properties of the object. Object relationships are used to define parameter value constraints. In Object Oriented Design (OOD), analysts and designers employ a variety of rules to identify objects (Booch, 1991). This specialized domain analysis

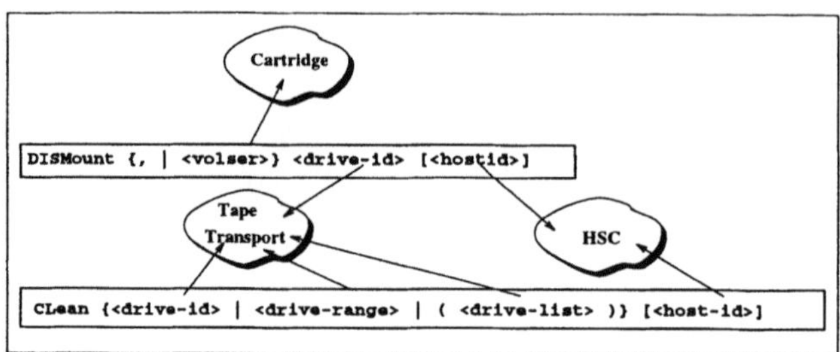

Figure 3. Analyzing HSC Commands for Objects and Object Elements

focuses on *syntactic elements, user documentation,* and *user semantic interpretation* for object identification.

Step #1.1 identifies objects of the system under test. Each parameter in the command language is categorized according to the object it influences. This classification gives a first cut of the objects and their properties. Figure 3 shows how two HSC commands from the robot tape library have parameters that relate to three domain objects **Cartridge, Tape Transport,** and **HSC**.

The parameters within each object are *object elements*. Each object element is classified by defining its *object element type*. Object elements are similar to the concept of *object attributes* in OOA/OOD (Booch, 1991, Rubin and Goldberg, 1992), except that for testing, we do not need as much information about an object when compared to the amount of information needed to implement one.

Each object element is classified as a parameter or non-parameter of the command language. Object elements related to command language parameters can be *parameter attributes, mode parameters,* or *state parameters*. A parameter attribute uniquely identifies an object. Mode parameters set operating modes for the system under test. State parameters hold state information for the object. Sometimes domain analysts provide semantic information that cannot be found in the parameters of the command language. These object elements are called *non-parameters* and may be important for test case generation. A non-parameter event is an event caused by the dynamics and consequences of issuing a sequence of commands. A non-parameter state is state information that cannot be controlled through the command language.

Step #1.2 defines default parameter sets for each object element and creates two glossaries, the *object glossary* and the *object element glossary*. The object glossary maintains information about each object by recording its name, a short description, a list of commands associated with the object, and the names of its object elements. Table 2 shows the **LSM** entry from the Object Glossary.

Another glossary stores detailed information about each object element. To select parameter values, automated test generation must know the range of values for each element, the representation of each object element, and the default set of values for each object element. Table 3 shows an entry from the Object Element Glossary for the StorageTek HSC command language.

The next step in the domain analysis determines relationships between objects. These relationships are captured in an *object hierarchy* in the form of a structural or "part-of" hierarchy. Step #1.4 annotates the object hierarchy with parameter constraint rules which describe how the choice of one parameter value constrains the choices for another. For example (see Figure 4), each ACS supports up to sixteen LSMs (shown in the figure as an arrow from the ACS object to the LSM object). Each LSM contains panels, tape drives, cartridge access ports, etc. Arrows from the LSM to each object denote this structure. Annotations on the arcs state parameter constraint rules. For instance, the choice of an ACS (i.e., a specific *acs-id* value) constrains choices for the LSM (i.e., possible *lsm-id* values).

5.2. *Command definition*

Step #2 of the domain analysis defines command syntax and semantic rules for each command. Three types of semantic rules are defined for commands: *preconditions, postconditions*, and *intracommand rules*. Preconditions ensure proper state or mode for a command and may constrain valid parameter values. Postconditions state effects on object elements and influence future command sequences or parameter value selection. The third com-

Table 2. Object Glossary Entry for the **LSM** Object

Object	**LSM**
Description	Library Storage Module - A single tape "silo"
Commands	DISPLAY MODify MOVE VIew Warn
Parameter Attribute	*lsm-id*
Mode Parameter	*lsm-subpool-threshold* *lsm-scr-threshold*
Parameter State	*lsm-status*
Non-parameter Event	*lsm-full*
Non-parameter State	none

Table 3. **LSM Entry from the HSC Object Element Glossary**

Parameter Attribute	*lsm-id*
Full Name	Library Storage Module (LSM) Identifier
Definition	Names an Instance of an LSM within an ACS
Values	000...FFF
Object	LSM
Representation	Range of values

mand level semantic rule is called an *intracommand rule*. These rules identify constraints placed on parameter value selection within a command. To illustrate, user documentation for the StorageTek HSC MOVE command states, "when moving a tape within the same LSM, the source and destination panels must be different." The domain model captures this intracommand rule as: if (lsm$1=lsm$2) => (panel$1 $\neq$ panel$2).

5.3. Script definition

Step #3 describes dynamic system behavior by capturing rules for sequencing commands and by classifying commands from the problem domain. Sequencing information is necessary because arbitrarily ordering a list of commands rarely produces semantically correct test cases.

The first part of scripting analysis is to group related commands into *scripting classes*. Scripting classes can partition by function, object, or object element. Functional partitioning creates scripting classes that include commands that perform similar actions. For example, in the StorageTek domain, the *set-up* class includes all commands that perform system set

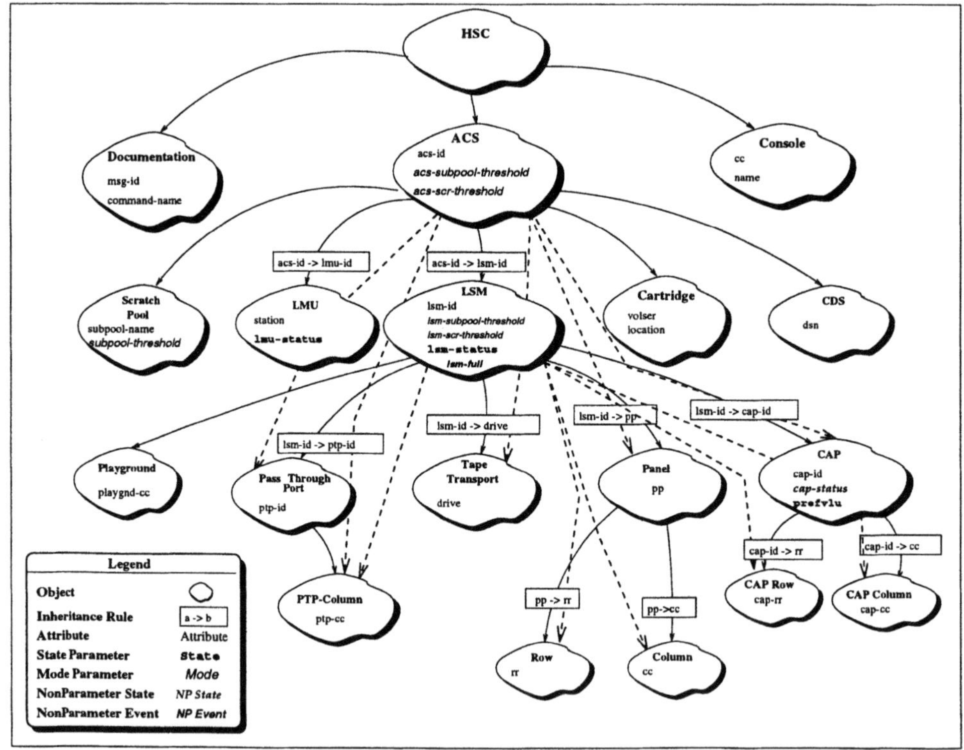

Figure 4. StorageTek Object Hierarchy

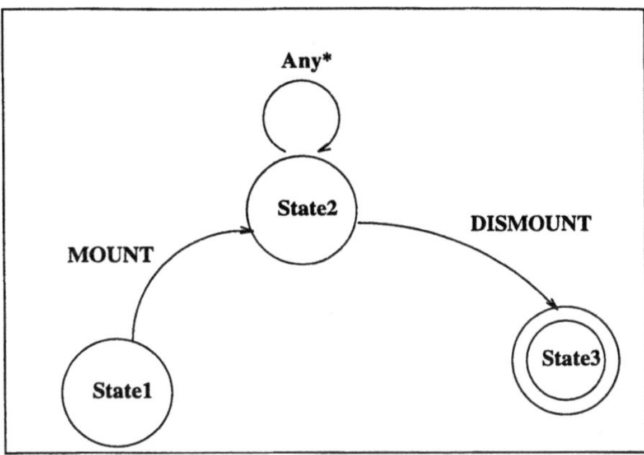

Figure 5. State Transition Diagram for the MOUNT-DISMOUNT Script Rule

Table 4. Script Rule: Parameter Value Selection

Rule	Description
p*	Choose any valid value for p
p	Choose a previously bound value for p
p-	Choose any except a previously bound value for p

up functions; the *action* class includes commands that manipulate and exercise the robot tape library. If we partition the commands by object, then we examine each object and create a class that contains all commands that influence that object.

Step #3.2 of the scripting analysis defines command sequencing rules. The results from this step include command sequencing information (i.e., script rule) and parameter binding information for each rule. For example, in the robot tape library, tapes must be mounted before they can be dismounted. Scripts are visualized as state transition diagrams (see Figure 5). Arcs are labelled with the names of specific commands or script classes. By restricting the commands that can be executed on each arc, we can create proper command sequences.

A command sequence can be annotated with parameter selection rules, as shown in Table 4. The first rule, $p*$, states that the value for parameter p can be selected from any valid choice as long as it fulfills parameter constraint rules. The second rule, p, restricts the value of parameter p to a previously bound value. The third rule, $p-$, denotes that parameter p can be selected from any valid choice except for the currently bound value of p. To illustrate, the MOUNT -> DISMOUNT sequence is annotated with script parameter selection rules.

```
MOUNT tape-id* drive-id*
Any*
DISMOUNT tape-id drive-id
```

This rule states that the *tape-id* and *drive-id* parameters can be selected from any valid choice for the MOUNT command while the DISMOUNT command must use the previously bound value for the *tape-id* and the *drive-id* parameters. Simply stated, the tape that is mounted in a drive should be dismounted from the same drive.

6.   Test Generation in Sleuth and UCPOP

The two approaches were developed from the StorageTek domain analysis. The Application Domain Based Testing method was implemented in *Sleuth*, an automated test generation tool developed at Colorado State University. The AI planning approach was implemented in UCPOP augmented by Lisp code.

Sleuth supports Domain Based Testing by providing tools and utilities for test generation. The main window directs the test generation process (see figure 6). *Sleuth* provides utilities to create domain models, configure test subdomains, and to generate tests. *Sleuth* is designed to maximize reuse of commands at all levels of abstraction (von Mayrhauser et al., 1994b), simplify uniform testing across configurations and versions, and support regression testing (von Mayrhauser et al., 1994a).

In this section, *Sleuth* and the planner implementation are described in terms of their architectures and knowledge representations. The two approaches are compared in terms of the test cases they generate and their basic capabilities.

6.1.   Architectures

6.1.1.   Sleuth Architecture

Sleuth is based on the Test Generation Process Model (shown in figure 7). The domain model, D_0^v, captures the syntax and semantics of the system under test. Tests generated from D_0^v are "valid" sequences of commands that follow all syntax and semantic rules in the domain model. Often, the domain model is modified to test a specific system configuration or to test a particular feature of the system under test. This creates a *test subdomain*, TSD_j^v, one for each modification j. *Test Criteria* influence the test subdomain definition and the test generation steps. Test engineers use their knowledge to modify the domain model. They also guide test generation by recalling archived test suites, identifying how many commands to generate, and what commands to generate.

Test Generation uses the test subdomain and instructions from the test engineer to create test suites, T_j^v. A *test suite* for DBT may contain *test cases*, *test templates*, and *test scripts*. A test case is a list of fully parameterized commands from the syntax of the problem domain. A test template is a list of commands with place holders for parameters. Test scripts are lists of command names.

As shown in figure 6, *Sleuth* uses a three stage test generation process. In the first stage, script classes and script rules are expanded. This produces a list of command names. The second stage creates a command template. Parameters remain as place holders. The last

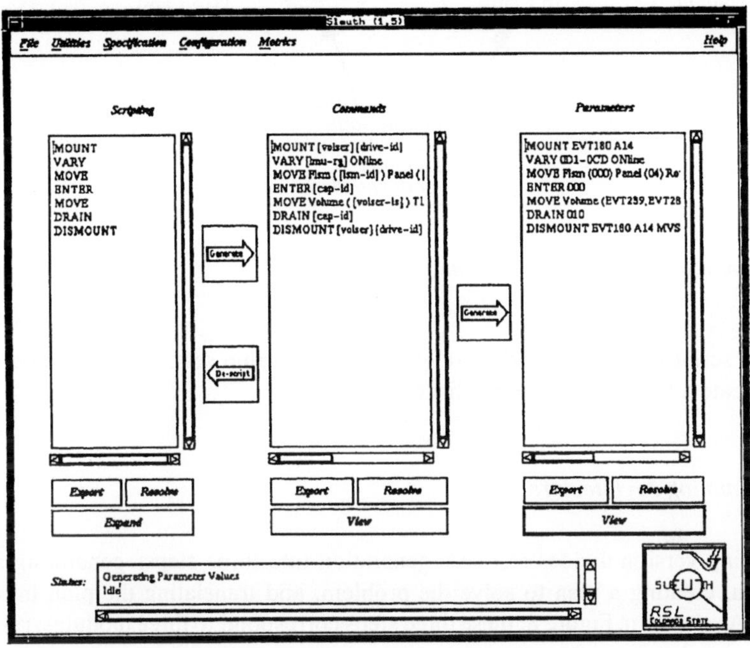

Figure 6. Window Based Test Generation Tool

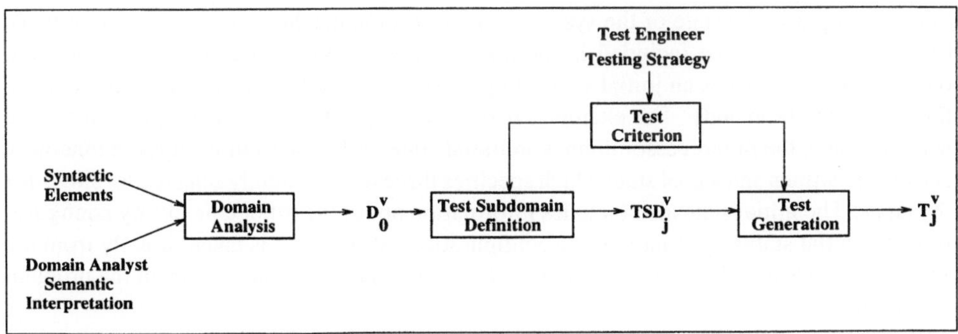

Figure 7. Test Generation Process Model

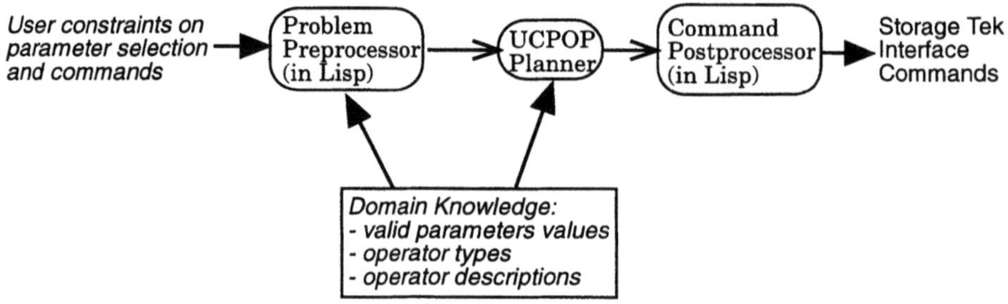

Figure 8. Sequence for generating test cases using UCPOP

stage uses script parameter binding rules, parameter value sets, and parameter constraint rules to create a fully parameterized list of commands.

6.1.2. *Planning Architecture*

The planning version divides test case generation into three steps: generating a problem description, creating a plan to solve the problem, and translating the plan into test case notation. As shown in Figure 8, these three steps correspond to three modules, respectively: preprocessor, planner and postprocessor.

The preprocessor develops a problem description based on user directions. The problem description consists of a problem name, domain knowledge, an initial state and a goal state. The problem name is generated automatically. The domain is the knowledge base that describes the commands in the language. The knowledge base is described in section 6.2.2; ways of manipulating the knowledge base are described in section 7. The initial and goal states define the specific needs of a particular test case.

The preprocessor incorporates knowledge about how command language operations relate to changes in the state of the system. The user indicates how many of different types of operations should be included in the plan. Based on knowledge of the test domain, the preprocessor creates an initial state and goal state description that would require using the indicated commands. For example, if the user requests three move operations to be accomplished, the preprocessor defines an initial state with at least three tapes in randomly selected positions and a goal state which specifies three new randomly selected locations for the tapes. The initial state also includes information about the robot tape library configuration and initial status information; the configuration information is taken directly from the knowledge base and the initial status information is randomly generated from the problem constraints.

The planner, UCPOP, constructs a plan to transform the initial state into the goal state. If a plan cannot be found within a set amount of time, then the planner fails. In this case, we try a different initial state and goal state that satisfies the user's requirements. Because UCPOP is a fairly simple and inefficient planner, more complex and demanding problem

Table 5. Domain Model Components and Hybrid Representation

Domain Model Component	Hybrid Representation
Script Classes	Sets of Command Names
Script Sequencing Rules	Macro Expansion
Script Parameter Binding	Macro Expansion
Command Language Syntax	Syntax Diagrams
Command Preconditions	Implicit representation
Command Postconditions	Implicit representation
Intracommand Rules	First Order Logic
Parameter Constraint Rules	Parameter Value Sets Parameter Constraints based on Set Operations

descriptions are more likely to fail. Because this is a prototype, we did not attempt to improve UCPOP's performance on our problems.

The postprocessor translated from UCPOP's plan representation to the HSC syntax. The transformation was purely syntactic and relatively straightforward.

UCPOP is written in Lisp. Thus, the supporting code was written in Lisp and could create data structures for UCPOP, run UCPOP and access and modify the return values from UCPOP. The declarative nature of the representations in Lisp expedited automatically modifying the knowledge base and so changing the nature of the kinds of test cases generated.

6.2. *Knowledge Representation*

6.2.1. *Sleuth Representations*

Sleuth uses a hybrid domain model representation (see Table 5) during test generation.

Script Representation

Scripts capture dynamic behavior of the system under test. We represent three categories: Script Classes, Script Rules, and Script Parameter Binding. A scripting class helps testers select *what type* of commands should be generated for a test case. A command can be a member of more than one class; the number of classes and the types of script classes is problem dependent. The experimental subdomain for this research used the commands in Table 6 and assigned them to three script classes. The Any class contains all commands. Set-up commands perform machine set-up. Action commands cause physical actions within the ACS.

For script rules, macro expansion ensures that commands are sequenced properly. For example, in the robot tape library, one cannot "dismount" a tape from a tape drive unless one has previously been "mounted." The macro representation for this rule is: MOUNT <List of Commands> DISMOUNT. *Parameter binding* makes sure the parameters in the command sequence are meaningful. For instance, parameter binding information ensures that the tape that is "mounted" is the same tape that is "dismounted." This implicitly

Table 6. Commands and Script Classes for the StorageTek Experimental Subdomain

Command Name	Description	Script Class	
Dismount	Dismount a tape from a tape drive	Any	Action
Display	Display information to the console	Any	Action
Drain	Release the Cartridge Access Port	Any	Action
Eject	Eject tapes through CAP	Any	Action
Enter	Enter tapes through CAP	Any	Action
Modify	Turn an LSM Online or Offline	Any	Set-Up
Mount	Mount a tape in a tape drive	Any	Action
Move	Move a tape within an ACS	Any	Action
Srvlev	Set system service level	Any	Set-Up

handles preconditions and postconditions in the domain model as they relate to command sequencing.

Command Representation

The second component of the domain model captures the syntax and semantic rules for each command. Command syntax is needed to generate a command from the command language. *Sleuth*'s representation uses syntax diagrams for each command and a random-walk through the syntax creates an instance of a command.

Intracommand rules identify constraints placed on parameter value selection within a single command. These rules are represented in the domain model in first-order logic.

Parameter Representation

Parameters of the command language are represented as Parameter Value Sets. Using the set operations of Union, Intersection, and Difference, a variety of parameter sets can be defined. During test generation, parameter values may be constrained. For example, the value for a particular LSM (*lsm-id*) constrains possible values for panels, rows, and columns for cartridge storage. Parameter constraint rules are represented using a "parameter" hierarchy that denotes relationships between "parameters" and set operations to modify parameter value sets from which the test suite generator may select.

6.2.2. Planning Representations

UCPOP provides its own representations for planning operators; in addition, we represented domain knowledge in structures, lists and procedures in Lisp to support the pre- and post-processors. Table 7 lists each domain model component and its planning representation; each one is described subsequently.

Script Representation

A script class is represented as the planner's domain. In UCPOP, the domain is simply a list of operator definitions. In the experimental subdomain, the list contains eighteen operations: four versions of the move command, eject, enter, connect, servicetofull, servicetobase, modifytooff, modifytoon, drain, mount, dismount, and four versions of the display command.

Table 7. Domain Model Components and AI Planner Representation

Domain Model Component	Planner Representation
Script Classes	Collection of Planner Operators
Script Sequencing Rules	Operator preconditions
Script Parameter Binding	Operator effects
Command Language Syntax	Operators : One operator for each "path" in a command. Postprocessor : Translates Planner output into Command Language Syntax.
Command Preconditions	Operator preconditions
Command Postconditions	Operator effects
Intracommand Rules	Operator preconditions
Parameter Constraint Rules	Preprocessor : Initial State Generator Preprocessor : Goal Generator Preprocessor: supporting data structures

```
;;Description : Mount a tape in a tape drive.
;;Precondition : Service-Level = FULL.
;;                      Tape is inside the LSM.
;;                      LSM-status = ONLINE.
;;Postcondition: Tape is in the tape drive.
(define    (operator mount)
           :parameters ((loc ?slsm) ?vid ?m_did ?p ?c ?r )
           :precondition (and (full slev)(in ?vid ?slsm ?p ?r ?c)(on ?slsm))
           :effect (and (at ?vid ?m_did)(not(in ?vid ?slsm ?p ?r ?c))))


;;Description : Dismount a tape from a tape drive.
;;Precondition : Service-Level FULL
;;                      Tape is in the tape drive.
;;Postcondition: Tape is placed into the LSM.
(define    (operator dismount)
           :parameters(?vid ?m_did ?d_did ?p ?c ?r)
           :precondition(and (full slev)(at ?vid ?m_did)(eq ?m_did ?d_did))
           :effect (and (not (at ?vid ?m_did))(backtolsm ?vid through ?d_did)
                      (in ?vid unknown unknown unknown unknown)))
```

Figure 9. Planning representations of the Mount and Dismount commands

Script sequencing rules and parameter binding together legislate the correct ordering of commands. The AI planning representation includes this information implicitly in the preconditions and effects of the planner operators. For example, one sequencing rule requires that MOUNT precede DISMOUNT, which is implemented with the planner operators listed in Figure 9. Preconditions for DISMOUNT require a tape to be in a tape drive. A tape can be placed into a drive in one of two ways: (1) a tape can be in the tape drive in the initial state, or (2) the tape can be loaded as an *effect* of the MOUNT operator.

```
;;Description  : Change Service-Level to FULL.
;;Precondition : None.
;;Postcondition: Service-Level = FULL.
(define    (operator servicetofull)
              :precondition (base slev)
              :effect (and(not(base slev))(full slev)))


;;Description : Change Service-Level to BASE.
;;Precondition : None.
;;Postcondition: Service-Lever = BASE.
(define    (operator servicetobase)
              :precondition (full slev)
              :effect (and (not (full slev)) (base slev)))
```

Figure 10. Example planning representations of the command language syntax: changing service level

Command Representation

The next domain model component is the command language syntax. Unlike the grammar based methods, the AI planner does not explicitly represent the syntax of the command language. Instead, each path through a command is represented as a separate planning operator. A path through a command differs primarily in the type and number of parameters for the command. Thus, the resulting plan operators may differ in their parameters, possible parameter values and preconditions. For instance, the StorageTek command language uses the SRVLEV command to "toggle" the system's service level: service-level-cmd ::= SRVLEV {BASE | FULL}. As seen in Figure 10, two operators encode the command for the planner: one to change to "full" and the other to change to "base". To implement the toggling effect, the precondition is that the current level must be other than the value to which it is being set.

Each planning operator is represented in a form similar to the command syntax (i.e., same number and type of parameters but formatted in the planner's representation). In the case of the two service level commands, the planning action SERVICETOFULL is converted to the StorageTek command SRVLEV FULL. A postprocessor translates the planner output into the correct syntax.

The next three domain model components are command preconditions, command post-conditions, and command intracommand rules. All three are represented as preconditions and effects of planner operators. A command language precondition denotes sequencing information based on system state (in contrast to the script sequencing rules which are not assumed to involve system state). If the system is not in the correct state, the precondition provides information to put the system in the proper state. Likewise, command language postconditions specify how the state of the system changes upon executing an operator. For a command to be included in a valid plan, its preconditions must be satisfied by the initial state or by the effects of an action that precedes it.

Intracommand rules are also specified as preconditions to planner operators. These pre-conditions check parameter values within the command. Figure 11 shows one version of the

```
;;Description : Move a volume in a specific location to the destination LSM,panel.
;;Precondition : Source and destination LSM are online.
;;                    Service level is full.
;;                    Volume location is specified by LSM, panel,row,column.
;;                    Source and destination LSMs are connected.
;;Intracommand : Source and destination LSMs must be equal.
;;                    Source and destination panels must be different.
;;Postcondition: Move the volume to a new panel inside the same LSM.


(define    (operator movefour)
           :parameters ((loc ?slsm) ?sp ?sc ?sr (loc ?dlsm) ?dp ?dc ?dr (tape ?vid))
           :precondition (and (full slev)(on ?slsm)(on ?dlsm)
                              (eq ?slsm ?dlsm) (neq ?sp ?dp)
                              (in ?vid ?slsm ?sp ?sr ?sc)
                              (eq ?dc unknown) (eq ?dr unknown))
           :effect (and (from ?vid ?slsm ?sp ?sr ?sc ?dlsm ?dp ?dr ?dc)
                        (in ?vid ?dlsm ?dp ?dr ?dc)
                        (not (in ?vid ?slsm ?sp ?sr ?sc))))
```

Figure 11. Example planning representation of the command preconditions, postconditions and intracommand rules: move a volume

MOVE command, which encodes the previously discussed intracommand rule by requiring slsm (source LSM) and dlsm to be equal (eq) and sp (source panel) and dp (destination panel) to be not equal (neq). Another version of the move command covers the case in which the LSM's differ.

Parameter Representation

The last domain model component represents command language parameters and parameter constraints. The AI planner uses two components of the preprocessor to capture this information: Initial State Generator and Goal Generator. The initial state generator creates an initial state vector for the planning system by randomly choosing from options constrained by the user's goals and the parameter constraints. Parameter constraints are represented declaratively where possible and procedurally where necessary. For example, the configuration of the LSMs (their panels, rows, columns, etc.) are represented in structures and lists; the relationship of the variables in the configurations (e.g., panels have rows and columns) is represented in the preprocessing code.

In the StorageTek experimental subdomain, we concentrated on two test generation goals: Moving tapes and Mounting/Dismounting tapes. Therefore, all state information necessary for these experiments was included in the state vector. Figure 12 shows an example of an initial state which includes basic system status (e.g., service level), configuration (e.g., three LSM locations are available) and inventory (e.g., one tape is in LSM 10).

The second preprocessor uses object and parameter constraint information to generate a goal for the planner. A single goal for these experiments is to move an individual tape, to mount/dismount a single tape, or display information. If more than one command is needed, a conjunctive goal is created. An example of a compound goal is shown in

initial-state =	((BASE SLEV) (LOC 0) (ON 0) (CAP 0 ENTERING) (LOC 1) (OFF 1) (CAP 1 ENTERING) (LOC 10) (OFF 10) (CAP 10 ENTERING) (CONNECT 0 1) (TAPE EVT297)(IN EVT297 10 UNKNOWN UNKNOWN UNKNOWN))
goal =	(AND (FROM EVT280 0 UNKNOWN UNKNOWN UNKNOWN 1 UNKNOWN UNKNOWN UNKNOWN) (FROM UNKNOWN 0 1 2 3 0 4 5 6))

Figure 12. Example planning representation of objects, object elements and parameter constraints: initial state list and goal list

Figure 12. This compound goal was generated based on a request to create a test case with two tape movements in it. The fields in the goal statement are:

```
(FROM [tape-id] [src  lsm] [src  panel] [src  row] [src  column]
                [dest lsm] [dest panel] [dest row] [dest column])
```

The first subgoal requests the system to move tape EVT280 from LSM 000 to LSM 001. In this goal, we are not concerned about where the tape is located. We are only concerned about moving it to a different LSM. In the second subgoal, a tape located in panel 1, row 2, and column 3 is moved within the same LSM to panel 4, row 5, and column 6. These two examples show how testers can focus test generation at different levels of abstraction through planning system goals.

6.3. *Example Test Cases*

The planner based generator and Sleuth produce qualitatively different test cases. Sleuth generates commands from user directions on number and type and primarily by resolving sequencing rules with macro expansion and by making choices at points in a grammar; the planner version generates initial and goal states from choices based on user directions on number and type of commands and by generating a legal sequence of actions to achieve the selected goals.

Table 8 shows test cases generated by both systems when they were asked for a test case with a move command. The solution formulated by *Sleuth* generates a sequence of MODIFY commands. The first two perform useful work, but the third is redundant because *Sleuth* does not maintain state information. The ENTER command is a result of *Sleuth*'s random command selection. The ENTER command requires a sequencing rule: ENTER followed by one or more other commands followed by a DRAIN. Command #5 finally issues the MOVE command as required. The last two commands complete the test case. StorageTek testers interpret test cases like this from the point of view of testing a *shared device*. While this test case seems to have redundant or extraneous commands, the testers consider the sequence a merged list of instructions from multiple users.

Table 8. Comparing *Sleuth* and UCPOP Tests

	Sleuth Test Case	UCPOP Test Case
1	MODIFY 001 ONline	MODIFY 000 ONLINE
2	MODIFY 000 ONline	SRVLEV FULL
3	MODIFY 000 ONline	DRAIN 000
4	ENTER 000	ENTER 000
5	MOVE (EVT289) Tlsm(000)	MOVE VOLUME(EVT280) Tlsm(001)
6	MODIFY 001 ONline	
7	DRAIN 000	

The UCPOP test case must be generated in the context of the initial state and the goal. The initial state sets LSM 000 offline, Service level to Base, CAP 000 to Entering, and tape EVT280 located outside the ACS. The goal was to move a particular tape to LSM 001. The first two commands issued by the planner adjust the state of the system such that other commands are meaningful and can be executed. The DRAIN command is necessary because the initial state of the CAP is Entering. Since the CAP is a shared device, it must be released by the DRAIN command first. The ENTER command is important because tape EVT280 is currently located outside the robot tape library. After the tape is entered, the system issues the MOVE and achieves the goal. The UCPOP test case is shorter and more focused than the Sleuth case.

The planner's test cases incorporate more assumptions about the state of the system and compose the test cases based on different criteria. For example, Figure 13 shows a simple example of a test case developed by the planner and supporting code and represented in UCPOP's language. In response to a request for a test case with one dismount and one display command, the preprocessor generates an initial state with a tape, EVT297, located in LSM 010 (IN EVT297 10 16 7 23) and its LSM online (ON 10). The goal is to display a console status report about the LSM and to move the tape from tape drive A36 to its LSM. UCPOP's solution is listed in steps 1-3, and the postprocessor output is listed last. In this case, to generate a dismount, a tape must be in the drive, so a mount command is generated first. Each step is listed with its preconditions and each precondition is prefaced by the step number that satisfies it (a zero indicates it is satisfied by the initial state). Thus, a minimal plan for the test case requirements is three steps because the required preconditions concerning status are all fulfilled by the initial state. The postprocessor examines each step and generates the correct syntax for the StorageTek Robot Tape Library.

6.4. *Comparison of Capabilities*

We implemented 18 operators in the planning system which correspond to 9 commands in the StorageTek domain. In the *Sleuth* representation, the 9 commands required 9 syntax diagrams, 4 scripting rules, 1 intracommand rule, and eleven parameter files. We compared the two approaches in three ways: how much effort was required for model development

```
Initial:          ((FULL SLEV) (LOC 0) (OFF 0) (CAP 0 DRAINED) (LOC 1) (OFF 1)
                  (CAP 1 DRAINED) (LOC 10) (ON 10) (CAP 10 ENTERING) (CONNECT 0 1)
                  (LOC ACS) (TAPE EVT297) (IN EVT297 10 16 7 23))

Step 1:           (MOUNT 10 EVT297 A36 16 23 7) Created 2
                  0 -> (IN EVT297 10 16 7 23)
                  0 -> (LOC 10)
                  0 -> (ON 10)
                  0 -> (FULL SLEV)
Step 2:           (DISPLAY2 0) Created 3
Step 3:           (DISMOUNT EVT297 A36 A36 ?P1 ?C1 ?R1) Created 1
                  0 -> (FULL SLEV)
                  1 -> (AT EVT297 A36)

Goal:             (AND (CONSOLEMSG DISPLAY2 0)
                       (BACKTOLSM EVT297 THROUGH A36))

Postprocessor:

step 1 is:        (MOUNT EVT297 A36)
step 2 is:        (DISPLAY LSM 010)
step 3 is:        (DISMOUNT EVT297 A36)
```

Figure 13. Example Results from UCPOP : Goal = Display console message about LSM and replace a tape from tape drive A36 back to the LSM

and test generation, whether the test cases covered similar aspects of the domain, and what kinds of test cases were generated by the planning system.

Although the representation language required by the planner was unfamiliar to those programming the test cases, the planner implementation progressed fairly easily and resulted in remarkably little code. The bulk of the implementation was done by Li Li, an undergraduate who had no background in AI, but some in Software Engineering, over a 12 week period which included learning about domain based testing, *Sleuth* and AI Planning. Of course, this rapid development was expedited by the fact that the domain was well understood and had already been implemented in *Sleuth*.

UCPOP required very little "code" to represent the experimental subdomain. The two preprocessors, one postprocessor, and 18 operators needed 414 lines of code. For *Sleuth*, the entire test generation tool required about 25,000 lines of C (internals and Motif interface). However, *Sleuth* implemented a much larger test domain than UCPOP and included utilities for domain model definition, test subdomain configuration, metrics, and a sophisticated user interface. Despite the small code size in the planner, computation time for a test case could take from minutes to hours due to the inefficiency of the underlying planner.

We compared the domain coverage of the planning and *Sleuth* implementations by considering how each represented the seven levels of the domain model (as appear in Table 5). Both the *Sleuth* and planner representations employed similar mechanisms to implement

Script Classes. The *Sleuth* representation stores command names in a set, and the planner includes or excludes operators to form script classes.

Scripting Rules (sequencing rules and parameter bindings) require different approaches in the two representations. The *Sleuth* scheme needs command sequencing information in the first stage of test generation but it does not need parameter binding information until the last stage. The AI planner includes sequencing information and parameter binding rules in each operator.

The Command Syntax is represented differently in the two test generation engines. The planning system encodes each "path" through a command as a separate operator. One operator could represent multiple paths so long as all paths use the same parameters, the same preconditions, and produced the same effects; UCPOP allows some flexibility in the preconditions but little in the definition of the effects[1]. The test case is generated using a postprocessor to translate the UCPOP output into the appropriate StorageTek syntax. *Sleuth* stores each command as a syntax diagram and takes a random-walk through the syntax diagram to create a command template.

Command Preconditions and Postconditions are not explicitly represented in the *Sleuth* representation. They are either implicit in the script rule macros or testers must issue set up commands or execute a list of commands to put the system in the correct state. *Sleuth* does not keep track of non-parameter state information. The planner was able to represent pre/post conditions in each planning system operator. The trade off between these two representations is in the amount of state information required during test generation.

Parameter value sets and parameter constraints are handled differently in both domain model representations. *Sleuth* uses parameter value files, set definitions, and set operations. The default values for a parameter are defined using sets and set operations. If one parameter value constrains the choices for another, additional set operations allow *Sleuth* to choose from a constrained set. In the planning system, all parameter information was encoded into the preprocessor, which uses information about default parameter values and parameter constraint rules to define initial states and goals that do not violate the parameter selection rules.

One of the most interesting aspects of our results were the differences between the planning approach and the *Sleuth* approach to test data generation. Testers take different views of the problem during test generation. Using *Sleuth*, the tester focuses on what subset of commands to generate and how many commands. Using the planner, the tester describes the desired *outcome* and allows the planner to choose the appropriate sequence of commands to achieve the goal. We view planner based (goal oriented) test generation as a natural way to generate tests.

An unexpected result of our comparisons was the kind of tests that were generated. The planner can potentially "discover" unusual command sequences to achieve the goal. This is beneficial in test data generation because obvious approaches get tested most often and therefore find few or no faults. Unusual command sequences may achieve the same goal but uncover faults from command sequences that were not considered. For instance, one of our experiments required UCPOP to move a tape from one LSM to another. Instead of generating a MOVE command, it EJECTed the tape from one LSM and ENTERed it into the next. While this is a simple example, it shows how the planner can create innovative test sequences that the test engineers may not think about.

7.   Extensions to the Basic System

Test generation systems should be flexible enough to accommodate a variety of test intents and testing criteria. Therefore, the extensions to the basic planning system included capabilities for testing against a variety of common testing criteria. Usually, testers test both valid and invalid cases. Testers may want to focus testing on particular parts of the system (a specific testing subdomain) for a variety of testing objectives: testing a particular (set of) objects, testing specific commands, regression testing (testing new features and making sure that nothing was broken), or testing specific configurations (represented as subsets of values in the domain model). At other times, testers may need to test all possible values of a specific parameter (e.g., a parameter reflecting possible tape media). Testers may or may not be concerned about the order in which parameter values are chosen. This section illustrates how these testing objectives can be achieved with *Sleuth* and with the Planning system UCPOP. *Sleuth* provides test subdomain utilities for this purpose. For the planning system, operator descriptions are declarative and accessible from Lisp; thus, functions are easily built that modify the underlying knowledge base.

7.1.   *Invalid Test Cases*

For systems with a command language as a user interface, invalid cases can represent themselves in a variety of ways from testing erroneous syntax and violating rules of proper behavior (violating scripting rules and intracommand rules in the script) to purposely generating invalid parameter values, either by using values that are always invalid, or by generating values that are invalid in a specific context (e.g., values that violate parameter inheritance rules). This type of testing concentrates on the syntax of the command language and tests the error recovery capabilities of the parser. It also tests error recovery code related to semantically erroneous commands.

In *Sleuth*, one can turn off scripting and intracommand rules, making it possible to generate dynamically invalid command sequences interspersed with semantically correct command sequences. If a tester wants only sequences that violate rules of proper behavior, a *Sleuth* utility allows editing the rules (modification or negation) which would then guarantee breaking of the rules in specific ways and thus test error recovery code of the system under test. We can also edit the syntax with mutation operations. This causes commands with incorrect syntax to be generated. Similarly, parameter value utilities allow the tester to define parameter values that are invalid and to modify parameter inheritance rules so they violate the actual domain's.

We can duplicate these capabilities in the AI Planner version. Scripting and intracommand rules are built into the preconditions of the planner. Thus, the first mechanism for generating invalid test cases is to identify such preconditions and either remove or change them. For example, one scripting rule is that DISMOUNT should be proceeded by MOUNT. If the

Test Case A	Test Case B	Test Case C

DISMOUNT EVT280 A36
ENTER 010
SRVLEV FULL
MOUNT EVT289 A29
	MODIFY 001 ONLINE
	MODIFY 010 ONLINE
	MOVE FLSM(01) PANEL(19) ROW(14)
	   COLUMN(10) TLSM(10)
	   TPANEL(UNKNOWN)
	EJECT 010 EVT289
	DRAIN 000
	ENTER 000
		MODIFY 001 ONLINE
		DRAIN 001
		ENTER 001
		MODIFY 000 ONLINE
		MOVE VOLUME (X12B&C)
		   TLSM (000)

Figure 14. Invalid test cases: a) removing scripting rules, b) invalidating intracommand rules, c) illegal parameter values

precondition that legislates that sequencing (i.e., that the tape be at the drive) is removed, then DISMOUNT may not be preceded by MOUNT, as is the case in figure 14a.

One of the intracommand rules for the domain dictates whether a destination and source LSM must be equal (or not) for particular types of MOVE commands. The preconditions for the different move operators include these constraints; thus, the intracommand rules can be invalidated by toggling the equality constraints in the operator descriptions. Doing so produces test cases that are no longer syntactically correct. Given this change to the operators and a request for a test case with a MOVE command, the planner version produced the test case in figure 14b, in which the MOVE command includes the value "unknown" for a panel.

Additionally, we can invalidate the parameter set used by the preprocessor. For example, we can generate invalid tape ids, ones composed of illegal character combinations (e.g., 123ABC, ABC, or !$#@&*), use these in the preprocessor and so generate illegal syntax, as in the tape number listed in figure 14c.

7.2. *Subdomains*

During feature testing with *Sleuth*, testers may decide to focus their testing efforts by excluding certain parts of the domain. This can take several forms: If scripting classes were defined around similar functions, a tester may decide to turn off commands in some classes, which ensures that these commands will never be generated. Similarly, if scripting classes were defined around objects (such as tapes in the HSC domain), then a tester may choose to turn off all but the commands in the tape scripting class (which contains all commands that operate on tapes).

Further, testers may want to subset the application domain by constraining possible values for parameter values (subsetting parameter value sets). *Sleuth* supports a parameter value editor. For example, in the HSC domain, testers may only have a limited supply of named tapes (and their associated tape-id parameter).

Test subdomains can also be generated by test criteria rules. An example of such rules are the regression testing rules of (von Mayrhauser et al., 1994a). The approach underlying these rules is to determine the changes made to the original domain (adding, deleting, and modifying commands and associated rules) and from there to determine which parts of the domain are affected and therefore should be regression tested. Regression testing rules define the regression testing subdomain based on the types of changes. (von Mayrhauser et al., 1994a) shows how to automate this for *Sleuth*.

With UCPOP, testers guide test case generation by loading or excluding portions of the operator set during the planner's initialization. For instance, the experimental subdomain focused on "moving" tapes within the tape library. By including or excluding certain "move" operators, we could change test case generation, produce different command sequences for similar goals, or focus on specific types of tape movement.

In UCPOP, the domain (the list of operators) is part of every problem definition. Thus, the domain can be changed dynamically to reflect desired subdomains. For example, we can search the knowledge base for which of the move operators require the destination and source LSMs to be equal and restrict the domain to only those move commands. Because the preprocessor is not given the information about the subdomain, it may be unable to generate test cases from the subdomain; in this case, it returns the best test case possible, which will be partially instantiated (i.e., some of the parameters will have no value) and will be incomplete (i.e., it will not include all the commands necessary to complete the desired goal).

7.3. *Partition Testing*

Partition testing (Goodenough and Gerhart, 1975, Hamlet and Taylor, 1990) includes all testing criteria that define equivalence classes of input values with the proviso that a set of tests is adequate if it contains tests with values from each of the equivalence classes. How equivalence classes are developed varies: white box testing criteria may define equivalence classes through branch or dataflow criteria. A black box criterion example is category partition testing (Ostrand and Balcer, 1988).

In *Sleuth*, parameter values can be grouped into sets, from which values may be selected. This provides an obvious mechanism for defining partitions. Rules regulate selecting specific sets (and thus values from them).

In the planner version, the preprocessor uses the parameter sets to generate the initial state description. If the parameter sets are changed, then the preprocessor generates different initial conditions, which conform to the testing criteria of the partition. For example, we may have three partitions of tape ids: legally named valid tapes, legally named invalid tapes and illegally named tapes. If we wish to generate test cases that move each type, then we can generate three problem descriptions with the preprocessor, each relying on a different set of tape ids, and then generate test cases for each problem description. Figure 15 lists an initial state description for each of the three types of tape ids; the primary difference in the test cases is the tape ids referenced.

7.4. *Other Testing Strategies*

On occasion, testers want to test all values of certain sets of parameter values. They may want to do this in order or according to some random permutation of the values. In *Sleuth*,

	Legal, Valid	Legal, Invalid	Illegal, invalid
Init	((FULL SLEV) (LOC 0) (ON 0) (CAP 0 DRAINED) (LOC 1) (OFF 1) (CAP 1 DRAINED) (LOC 10) (ON 10) (CAP 10 DRAINED) (CONNECT 0 1) (LOC ACS) (TAPE EVT185) (IN EVT185 1 10 5 13))	((FULL SLEV) (LOC 0) (OFF 0) (CAP 0 ENTERING) (LOC 1) (OFF 1) (CAP 1 ENTERING) (LOC 10) (ON 10) (CAP 10 DRAINED) (CONNECT 0 1) (LOC ACS) (TAPE SCR185) (OUT SCR185 ACS) (FROM SCR185 ACS UNKNOWN UNKNOWN UNKNOWN))	((FULL SLEV) (LOC 0) (ON 0) (CAP 0 DRAINED) (LOC 1) (ON 1) (CAP 1 ENTERING) (LOC 10) (OFF 10) (CAP 10 DRAINED) (CONNECT 0 1) (LOC ACS) (TAPE ABC) (IN ABC 0 4 2 3))
Goal	(FROM EVT185 1 10 5 13 1 19 unknown unknown)	(FROM SCR185 0 unknown unknown unknown 10 unknown unknown unknown)	(FROM ABC 0 4 2 3 10 4 unknown unknown)

Figure 15. Partition Testing Example: partitioning cases by tape values

value selection is currently random, but could easily be enhanced to include capabilities such as Maurer's probabilistic grammars (Maurer, 1990). Even so, setting the number of commands to be generated high enough will guarantee that all parameter values will be generated. While this will not be a minimal set (in terms of number of commands generated), it is sufficient. The random selection also assures that it will not be pathologically large.

As with partitioning, the preprocessor can step through parameter values as easily as through parameter sets. In each case, the top level function in the preprocessor (which is called "generate-problem") is called with modified values for the parameter sets; at present, these sets are stored as global variables. In the case of partitioning, a whole new set is substituted; for parameter value coverage, the code iterates over the set of values forcing a single one to be used in each test case that is generated.

8. Future Work

The planning based test case generator described in this paper is just a prototype, intended to assess whether the planning paradigm could generate interesting test sequences under a variety of test criteria. Our explorations indicate that the domain knowledge about testing is naturally represented in a planner and that the planner's representation and reasoning is flexible enough to support different testing criteria.

However, a number of questions remain about the long term viability of planning as a platform for automated test case generation. Can the planner be scaled up to larger test cases and a larger domain model? What extensions are necessary for this to be a useful tool for testers? What constitutes reasonable testing goals and should goal synthesis be automated as well?

On the question of scale up, we have already encountered difficulties in producing long test cases using the UCPOP planner. The planner is designed to be correct and complete, which means that if a solution is possible, UCPOP will find it *eventually*. Because it was designed as a theoretically and pedagogically interesting tool, its built-in search strategy is not efficient. We have alleviated that problem to some extent by incorporating more efficient general search strategies (Srinivasan, 1995), but these changes are not enough. We will explore two possibilities for expediting scale-up: including domain specific search strategies in UCPOP and transferring the knowledge base to another planner. Some preliminary explorations suggest that UCPOP is occasionally going down garden paths in the search space for this domain; domain specific strategies should eliminate those pathologies. If these strategies are inadequate for scale-up, then we will port the knowledge base to a more efficient planner which is, however, harder to program. The simplicity of UCPOP is attractive for expediting use by potential users.

In parallel with the search strategy effort, we will be implementing the full domain. Because the subset includes examples of all types of representation for the domain, we anticipate little problem with adding to the knowledge base.

On the question of encapsulating the planning version into a useful tool, the primary lack is a user interface. At present, all interactions are through a set of Lisp functions, useful for the developers who need to exert control, but awkward for any users. We will be building a menu and query driven interface in CLIM (Common Lisp Interface Manager) for the system. The composition of the interface (i.e., the options for the user) will depend in part on determining how user's testing goals should be accommodated.

The primary research question remaining is representing and automating goal generation. Our approach has been passive, requiring the user to indicate what should be done, and command oriented, requiring goals specified in terms of number and types of commands. Many other testing goals might be incorporated as well: focused testing of suspect parts of the system, coverage of parameter or command sets, or testing for interaction effects between sets of commands. These higher level goals could form the basis for strategic reasoning about test suites; at present, we reason only about single test cases. Generating criteria for test suites can be viewed as a higher level planning or search problem, making it conducive to solution by a variety of AI techniques (e.g., hierarchical planning, heuristic search or active learning). We need to enumerate the desired testing goals, acquire knowledge about when goal types are most appropriate and how test suite goals are manifest in individual test cases and incorporate test suite goal reasoning into the system and its interface.

Automated planning systems offer several potential advantages for test case generation. First, ordering the operations in the test case and checking that the order is correct is handled automatically by the planning system. Second, the representation is natural for describing commands and their interactions, information that is necessary for developing test cases. Third, the flexibility of describing new initial states and goal states makes it amenable to generating many different test cases for the same system. Finally, the full description required by the planner ensures that only correct cases will be generated. Conversely, should illegal test cases be desired, they can be generated relatively easily by "mutilating" the operator descriptions (e.g., removing parts of the preconditions or effects).

Planning for testing shows promise as a new method for automatically generating test cases. We have demonstrated its value on a realistic subset of an industrial testing domain. What remains is extending the method to larger sets and to test suites.

Acknowledgments

This research was partially supported by the Colorado Advanced Software Institute (CASI), StorageTek, the Air Force Institute of Technology, the CRA Mentoring Project, a Colorado State University Diversity Career Enhancement grant, and a National Science Foundation Research Initiation Award #RIA IRI-9308573. CASI is sponsored in part by the Colorado Advanced Technology Institute (CATI), an agency of the state of Colorado. CATI promotes advanced technology teaching and research at universities in Colorado for the purpose of economic development. The authors thank Li Li for implementing the system while working as a summer research assistant and anonymous reviewers for the 1995 Knowledge Based Software Engineering Conference for their pointers and comments.

Notes

1. This problem has been alleviated in UCPOP 4.0

References

Charles Anderson, Anneliese von Mayrhauser, and Rick Mraz. "On the Use of Neural Networks to Guide Software Testing Activities", *Procs. International Test Conference*, Oct. 1995, Washington, DC.

John S. Anderson. *Automating Requirements Engineering Using Artificial Intelligence Techniques*. PhD thesis, Dept. of Computer and Information Science, University of Oregon, Dec. 1993.

Anthony Barrett, Keith Golden, Scott Penberthy, and Daniel Weld. *UCPOP User's Manual*. Dept of Computer Science and Engineering, University of Washington, Seattle, WA, October 1993. TR 93-09-06.

J. Bauer and A. Finger. "Test Plan Generation Using Formal Grammars", *Procs. Fourth International Conference on Software Engineering*, 1979, pp. 425-432.

Franco Bazzichi and Ippolito Spadafora. "An Automatic Generator for Compiler Testing," *IEEE Transactions on Software Engineering*, 1982:8(4), pp.343-353.

Ted J. Biggerstaff and Alan J. Perlis. *Software Reusability: Volume I, Concepts and Models*, ACM Press, Fronier Series, 1989.

Grady Booch, *Object Oriented Design with Applications*, "Benjamin/Cummings", 1991.

A. Celentano, S. Crespi Reghizzi, P. Della Vigna, C. Ghezzi, G. Gramata and F. Savoretti. "Compiler Testing using a Sentence Generator," *Software-Practice and Experience*, 1980:10, pp.987-918.

John J. Chilenski and Philip H. Newcomb. "Formal Specification Tools for Test Coverage Analysis", *Procs. Ninth Knowledge-Based Software Engineering Conference*, September 1994, Monterey, CA, pp. 59-68.

Paul R. Cohen and Edward A. Feigenbaum. *Handbook of Artificial Intelligence*, volume 3, chapter Planning and Problem Solving, pages 513–562. William Kaufmann, Inc., Los Angeles, 1982.

A.G. Duncan and J.S. Hutchison, "Using Attributed Grammars to Test Designs and Implementations," *Proceedings of the Fifth International Conference on Software Engineering*, 1981, pp. 170-177.

Tsum S. Chow. "Testing Software Design Modeled by Finite State Machines," *Proceedings of the First COMPSAC*, 1977, pp. 58-64.

W. Deason, D. Brown, K.-H. Chang, and J. Cross. "Rule-Based Software Test Data Generator", *IEEE Transactions on Knowledge and Data Engineering*, 3(1), March 1991, pp. 108-117.

Stephen Fickas and John Anderson. A proposed perspective shift: Viewing specification design as a planning problem. Department of Computer and Information Science CIS-TR-88-15, University of Oregon, Eugene, OR, November 1988.

Stephen Fickas and B. Robert Helm. "Knowledge Representation and Reasoning in the Design of Composite Systems", *IEEE Transactions on Software Engineering*, SE-18(6), June 1992, pp. 470-482.

Tom Figliulo, Anneliese von Mayrhauser, and Richard Karcich. "Experiences with Automated System Testing and SLEUTH", *Procs. IEEE Aerospace Applications Conference 1996*, February 1996.

S. Fujiwara, G. von Bochman, F. Khendek, M. Amalou, and A. Ghedamsi. "Test Selection Based on Finite State Models", *IEEE Transactions on Software Engineering SE-17*, no. 10(June 1991), pp. 591-603.

J. B. Goodenough and S. L. Gerhart. "Toward a Theory of Test Data Selection", *IEEE Transactions on Software Engineering*, SE-1(2), June 1975, pp. 156-173.

Dick Hamlet and Ross Taylor. "Partition Testing Does not inspire Confidence", *IEEE Transactions on Software Engineering*, SE-16(12), Dec. 1990, pp. 1402-1411.

James W. Hooper and Rowena O. Chester. *Software Reuse: Guidelines and Methods*, Plenum Publishers, 1991.

Karen Huff and Victor Lesser. A plan-based intelligent assistant that supports the software development process. In *ACM SIGSOFT/SIGPLAN Software Engineering Symposium on Practical Software Development Environments*, Nov. 1988.

Karen Huff. Software adaptation. In *Working Notes of AAAI-92 Spring Symposium on Computational Considerations in Supporting Incremental Modification and Reuse*, pages 63–66, Stanford University, March 1992.

D. C. Ince. "The Automatic Generation of Test Data", *Computer Journal*, vol.30(1), 1987, pp. 63-69.

P. Maurer. "Generating Test Data with Enhanced Context-Free Grammars", *IEEE Software*, July 1990, pp. 50-55.

Glenford J. Myers. *The Art of Software Testing*, Wiley Series in Business Data Processing. John Wiley and Sons, 1979.

Thomas J. Ostrand and Marc J. Balcer. "The Category-Partition Method for Specifying and Generating Functional Tests", *Communications of the ACM*, 31(6), June 1988, pp. 676-686.

J.S. Penberthy and D. Weld. "UCPOP: A sound, complete, partial order planner for ADL", In *Proceedings Third International Conference on Principles of Knowledge Representation and Reasoning*, October 1992, pp. 103-114.

P. Purdom. "A Sentence Generator for Testing Parsers", *BIT*, 12(3), 1972, pp. 366-375.

Debra J. Richardson, Owen O'Malley, and Cindy Tittle. "Approaches to Specification-Based Testing", *Procs. ACM Third Symposium on Software Testing, Analysis, and Verification (TAV3)*, December 1993, pp. 86-96.

Robert S. Rist. Plan Identification and Re-use in Programs. In *Working Notes of AAAI-92 Spring Symposium on Computational Considerations in Supporting Incremental Modification and Reuse*, pages 67–72, Stanford University, March 1992.

Kenneth S. Rubin and Adele Goldberg. "Object Behavior Analysis," *Communications of the ACM*, 35(9), September 1992, pp. 48-62.

Raghavan Srinivasan and Adele E. Howe. Comparison of Methods for Improving Search Efficiency in a Partial-Order Planner. In *Proceedings of the 14th International Joint Conference on Artificial Intelligence*, pages 1620–1626, Montreal, Canada, August 1995.

StorageTek, *StorageTek 4400 Operator's Guide*, Host Software Component (VM) Rel 1.2.0, StorageTek, 1992.

Gerald A. Sussman. A computational model of skill acquisition. Technical Report Memo no. AI-TR-297, MIT AI Lab, 1973.

Markos Z. Tsoulakas, Joe W. Duran, and Simeon C. Ntafos. "On Some Reliability Estimation Problems in Random and Partition Testing", *IEEE Transactions on Software Engineering*, 19(7), July 1993, pp. 687-697.

Anneliese von Mayrhauser and Steward Crawford-Hines, "Automated Testing Support for a Robot Tape Library," *Proceedings of the Fourth International Software Reliability Engineering Conference*, November 1993, pp. 6-14.

Anneliese von Mayrhauser, Richard T. Mraz, and Jeff Walls. "Domain Based Regression Testing," *Proceedings of the International Conference on Software Maintenance*, Sept 1994, p. 26-35.

Anneliese von Mayrhauser, Richard Mraz, Jeff Walls, and Pete Ocken. "Domain Based Testing: Increasing Test Case Reuse," *Proc. of the International Conference on Computer Design*, October 1994, p. 484-491.

Anneliese von Mayrhauser, Jeff Walls, and Richard Mraz, "Testing Applications Using Domain Based Testing and Sleuth," *Proceedings of the Fifth International Software Reliability Engineering Conference*, November 1994, p. 206-215.

Anneliese von Mayrhauser, Jeff Walls, and Richard Mraz. "*Sleuth*: A Domain Based Testing Tool," *Proc. of the International Test Conference*, October 1994, p. 840-849.

Elaine J. Weyuker and Bingchiang Jeng. "Analyzing Partition Testing Strategies", *IEEE Transactions on Software Engineering*, 17(7), July 1991, pp. 703-711.

Steven J. Zeil and Christian Wild. "A Knowledge Base for Software Test Refinement", Technical Report TR-93-14, Old Dominion University, Norfolk, VA.

Automated Software Engineering, 4, 107–109 (1997)

Desert Island Column

WLADYSLAW M. TURSKI   wmt@mimuw.edu.pl

Institute of Informatics, Warsaw University, Banacha 2, 02-097 Warsaw, Poland

In the Desert Island Column, authors, marooned on a desert island, write about books and/or papers, relevant to software engineering, that they would value having with them above all others. They may be seminal, thought-provoking or simply a pleasure to read. In a slight change to the usual format of the column, Professor Wladyslaw Turski has chosen to write about a book he would write on a desert island. Ed.

Once upon a time, an otherwise very generous reviewer, in an otherwise very complimentary review of one of my books, obviously pained by the effort to consult many references quoted in it, suggested in exasperation that the author should be sent to a desert island, without any library sources, and made to write the book entirely from the memory. I found the idea quite appealing (provided, of course, the island would be somewhere in the South Pacific, and the shortage of literary nourishment would be compensated by other delights). So when asked to write a column on the books I would take with me to a desert island, I immediately seized the opportunity to invert the problem and - in the virtual reality of the exercise - to satisfy the good reviewer's request at least in a sketch form.

I would like to write a, or rather "the," book covering all that a software engineer should know. I do not want the book to be too fat, so simply adding together the contents of all courses normally taught for a degree in software engineering is out. Dare I eliminate any of the subjects? Considered separately, one by one, each seems far too important to be left out. But when I mentally scan their contents, I see much of the material gets repeated, albeit in different guises.

For instance, memory management (sharing, protection, swapping etc.) is discussed in compilers, operating systems, databases, networking ... The same few principles, algorithms and techniques are introduced as solutions to different problems, described in terms of these problems and, therefore, may appear different. This not only increases the volume of what we teach, but makes the teaching less useful by conditioning the student to associate particular versions of general principles directly with particular, isolated problems. Faced with yet another instance of the general problem, one that by chance was not treated in the courses they had taken, and being unaware of its general form (of its abstract statement), software engineers educated in this fashion may be tempted to consider an unfamiliar instance as a genuinely new problem. Depending on their intelligence, they can discover a solution, or give up struggling; in either case they suffer unnecessarily.

So in my book, I would write about these general principles of computer programming, and in exercises, or small-print comments, I would indicate particular, well-known practical problems that can be solved by application of these principles. There would be no need, for example, to make a lot of song and dance about object-oriented this or that. Concepts of class, rules of inheritance, discipline of feature accessing, extent of scoping, indeed, even principles of synchronization and mutual exclusion would be all introduced as basic properties of modularity. Any particular combination thereof would be then just a simplification, again deserving an exercise or a small-print case illustration.

(Quite early in my life I was taught Latin grammar. Ever since, I have had no real problem with any other grammar of an ethnic language: it was always just a case of learning which parts do not apply, and of absorbing some local terminology; no conceptual hurdles at all. My friends who were spared the "horrors" of learning Latin grammar, keep on struggling with grammars of each new language they try to pick up. It is only the brightest who for themselves invent a "transitive closure" of individual grammars they learned, form an abstract, universal grammar, which - give or take some inessential bits - turns out to be isomorphic with Latin grammar.)

The essence of programming and program implementation, inclusive, of course, of principles of the so-called specification and program correctness (i.e., semantic morphisms between formal texts), would constitute the hard core of the book. Together with exercises and small-print comments relating the principles to their various embodiments and trade names it would be also the main part of its bulk. The remainder would be devoted to two topics.

One would be a brief survey of the main extra-logical but measurable constraints on programs. Here I would treat the issues of computational complexity, system reliability and, perhaps, special requirements of real-time programming. All these relate to programs in execution; i.e., to the processes invoked in a computing device by program application. As with the programs themselves, a clear exposition of essential principles would lead to a reasonably compact presentation of these seemingly diverse, practically important subjects.

The final chapter of the book would be the software-construction process seen as an industrial undertaking. As there is not much scientific material to cover under this rubric (and the inaccessibility of library collections would prevent any attempt to hide ignorance behind details of case studies), I would concentrate on three fundamental observations and their consequences.

(1) The software is written primarily to be used by a client. The ultimate measure of its success is the client's satisfaction. This introduces the need to monitor (or, better still, to measure) the client's reaction, and use the thus obtained information for improving the entire process of software-making. In particular, to satisfy the client, the software may need to enjoy qualities other than just correctness. Such extra qualities may have to be designed into the software and into the process of its development as they hardly ever are of the add-on variety.

(2) The software construction process consists of a repeated application of the same pattern: a specification (a formal text) is implemented (transformed into another linguistic system), and the thus obtained formal text (a "program") becomes the specification for the next step. This pattern has rigid rules for actual implementation and a degree of flexible choice in deciding the target for the current implementation (the current target linguistic system). While the act of implementation is (at least in principle) mechanistic, the choice of target is the creative part. The main body of the book provides the mathematics to compute the mechanistic part; doing the creative part properly must be learned by experience.

(3) It appears that the software construction process is subject to constraints not entirely controlled at will by managerial techniques. It also appears that some parameters of the

inherent dynamics of this process, specific for a class of software-objects produced and a particular software producing organization, can be detected by judiciously chosen statistical observations. Relating changes in such parameters to changes in the organization it may be possible to infer how to improve the performance of the process.

I have just noted that listing the three observations I switched the style: from writing "about" the book to writing its text (well, portions of it). Upon a short reflection I decided to let it stand. It is yet another indication of how strongly different from the rest of the book is the subject matter of its planned final chapter. Unfortunately, with my present knowledge, I cannot even hope to achieve more homogeneity; on the other hand, none of these topics can be altogether avoided in a comprehensive book on software engineering.

In the books I have published so far (Turski, 1968, 1971, 1972, 1975, 1978, 1980, 1987), I tended to employ many different notational conventions, both in order to follow as closely as possible the specifics of each subject I was treating, and to convince the reader that the actual shape of the notation is quite irrelevant. In the book I would write on the island, having no access to the sources, I would have to give up this habit. The choice of notation would be a pleasant challenge. I have no doubt that in principle I would opt for a version of logic calculus; the choice of a specific one would be influenced by the aesthetic considerations: who knows how the island's environment would affect my perception of beauty.

References

Wladyslaw M. Turski, "Principles of Computer Use" (in Polish), PWN, Poland, 1968, sec. ed. 1973.

Wladyslaw M. Turski, "Data Structures" (in Polish), WNT, Poland, 1971, sec. ed. 1976, German translation: Akademie Verlag, 1975.

Wladyslaw M. Turski (editor), "Programming Teaching Techniques" North-Holland, 1972.

Wladyslaw M. Turski, "Informatics. A Propaedeutic View" (in Polish), PWN, 5 editions 1975 - 1989, English translation: North Holland, 1985.

Wladyslaw M. Turski, "Computer Programming Methodology", Heyden, 1978. Polish translation: WNT, 1978 and 1985; Russian translation: Mir, 1981.

Wladyslaw M. Turski, "Not by informatics alone" (in Polish), PIW, Poland, 1980.

Wladyslaw M. and T.S. Maibaum, "The Specification of Computer Programs", Addison-Wesley, 1987.